OF PARADISE AND
LIGHT

E. C. PETTET

OF PARADISE AND LIGHT

A STUDY OF VAUGHAN'S
SILEX SCINTILLANS

CAMBRIDGE
AT THE UNIVERSITY PRESS
1960

PUBLISHED BY

THE SYNDICS OF THE CAMBRIDGE UNIVERSITY PRESS

Bentley House, 200 Euston Road, London, N.W.1
American Branch: 32 East 57th Street, New York 22, N.Y.

©

CAMBRIDGE UNIVERSITY PRESS

1960

PRINTED IN GREAT BRITAIN BY ROBERT MACLEHOSE AND CO. LTD
THE UNIVERSITY PRESS, GLASGOW

But He that with His blood—a price too dear—
 My scores did pay,
Bid me, by virtue from Him, challenge here
 The brightest day;
Sweet, downy thoughts, soft lily-shades, calm streams,
 Joys full, and true,
Fresh, spicy mornings, and eternal beams,—
 These are His due.

THE RELAPSE

CONTENTS

PREFACE

In this study of Henry Vaughan's *Silex Scintillans,* which now and then also glances at some of his other and less important verse, I have tried to follow the critical ideal of combining the general and the particular, the long-range survey and the close-up scrutiny. I mention this fact because it explains the pattern of the book.

I would also briefly add, with particular reference to the middle section, that while I share many of T. S. Eliot's recently expressed views on the 'lemon-squeezer school of criticism', I believe too that we must vary our critical methods and our reader-responses from poet to poet. Because there is often so much multiple meaning, so much allusion and quotation, and so many fine threads of esoteric reference in Vaughan's poetry, we must read it with an exceptionally close attention and with a good deal of circumstantial knowledge if we are to share its experience, and enjoy it, to the full.

Texts for quotation always present something of a problem when one is writing about our older poets. For several reasons I have usually followed (with an occasional slight alteration) the modernised text of E. K. Chambers in the *Muses Library* edition of Vaughan's poetry in preference to L. C. Martin's authoritative *Vaughan's Works,* which is virtually a reprint of the originals. In Chapter XI, however, for the special purposes of that chapter, I have taken my quotations from Martin's edition. All the prose quotations, slightly modernised, are also from *Vaughan's Works.*

Biblical quotations are taken from the Authorized Version, and those from George Herbert follow (with one or two minor changes) the text of F. E. Hutchinson's *Works of George Herbert.*

Among those who have helped me in various ways I should particularly like to thank my friend and colleague, Mr D. D.

Brown, for his general and most encouraging interest in the work and for his practical and ever-ready assistance in trying to solve some of the teasing problems that cropped up from time to time.

WROTHAM, KENT
February 1959

E. C. P

PART I

THE SHAPING OF THE POETRY

CHAPTER I

FROM WITHIN

I N the achievement of *Silex Scintillans* Vaughan offers a remarkable instance of a poet who, after several years of earth-skimming, bare flight, suddenly soars up into the sky.

Nothing will ever fully explain that abrupt, steep ascent; nor will the likeliest explanations, in themselves, help us to enjoy and appreciate the poems any better. But—to say nothing of the irresistible challenge to our curiosity—some investigation of the mystery may be profitable even for purely literary reasons, since it is hardly possible to examine inspirational forces without at the same time engaging ourselves closely with the work that embodies them.

One conclusion at least may be stated with some measure of certainty. For all its immense superiority to the two volumes of mainly earlier poetry, *Poems* and *Olor Iscanus* (though these contain better work than Vaughan is often given credit for), *Silex Scintillans* is not some entirely new, inexplicable creation, without obvious antecedents. Rather—to use an inevitable metaphor where Vaughan is concerned—it is a transmutation of earlier poetic elements that have been subjected to a new fire and a new tincture.

For one thing, though there is frequently a mixture of styles, including much threadbare poetic cliché, in Vaughan's early work, the general run of the diction is not unlike that of *Silex Scintillans*—'commonplace words in a prose order': what the language lacks—admittedly an all-decisive difference—is the recurrent heightening and surprise of the 'startingly poignant phrase'.[1] Again, even if it is impossible to accept Marilla's con-

---

[1] Both quotations are from Mrs Joan Bennett, *Four Metaphysical Poets* (Second Edition), p. 86.

tention[1] that the lyrics of *Silex Scintillans* resemble the earlier secular ones in their structure and mode of development, there are certainly those important stylistic continuities, mainly of a metaphysical kind, that he notes—the dramatic type of opening, the backing of argument by scientific analogy, the use of parallels and antitheses, the common working up to a climax. Further, the secular poems are undoubtedly related to the religious ones by their use of images drawn from Nature, their occasional hermetic and allied references, and their sometimes marked rhetorical strain.[2]

However, what chiefly connects Vaughan's earlier and later work is his imagery; and it is no weakening of the argument for the organic continuity of his writing to lay special emphasis on this one particular resemblance, since, as we shall progressively see, imagery is of quite exceptional importance in his poems, in their inspiration, structure, and general effect.

Without any exaggeration we may say that most of the key-images of *Silex Scintillans*, admittedly without their later symbolical richness and complexity, are clearly prefigured in the earlier poems. For instance, the ubiquitous cloud and star is to be found in the description of the Globe Tavern's painted ceiling, which, if Vaughan's picture is real and not imaginary, may be counted among its origins :

> That artificial cloud, with its curl'd brow,
> Tells us 'tis late; and that blue space below
> Is fir'd with many stars.

A Rhapsodis

Again, the cognate image of the sun shining through or around some cloud is surely to be traced in the lines,

> But I past such dim mourners can descry
> Thy fame above all clouds of obloquy,
> And like the sun with his victorious rays
> Charge through that darkness to the last of days;

An Elegy on the death of Mr R. Hall

[1] 'The Secular and Religious Poetry of Henry Vaughan', *M.L.Q.*, vol. 9, no. 4 (Dec. 1948).
[2] See chap. XII.

while another elegy, *On the death of Mr R. W.*, contains something very like the paradox of the sun shining at midnight that we find in *The Night* and elsewhere :

> As some blind dial, when the day is done,
> Can tell us at midnight there was a sun.

Closely akin to the image of the cloud-masked sun there is that of the light of the soul veiled by the physical body, which can be seen, adumbrated at least, in some of the lines on the plays and poems of William Cartwright :

> Nor are those bodies they assum'd dark clouds,
> Or a thick bark, but clear transparent shrouds,
> Which who looks on, the rays so strongly beat
> They'll brush and warm him with a quick'ning heat.

(Incidentally, the last two lines of this quotation run close to a passage in *Cock-Crowing* :

> But brush me with Thy light, that I
> May shine unto a perfect day,
> And warm me at Thy glorious Eye!)

For the image of the dew that (among its other significations) is associated with tears of repentance, we may trace the most obvious line of continuity in transformation from the light-hearted description of Amyntas' mistress—

> Yet she, like flowers oppress'd with dew,
> Doth thrive and flourish in her tears—
>
> *Song*: 'Amyntas, go'

to the picture of St Mary Magdalen—

> Fresher than morning-flowers which show
> As thou in tears dost, best in dew.

Similarly the image of the shining ring of eternity, to be found in *The World* (ll. 1–3), *Vanity of Spirit* (ll. 3–6), *The Queer* (l. 3), and possibly in *Palm-Sunday* (ll. 20–3), is already intimated in *To Amoret Walking in a Starry Evening* :

> We might suspect in the vast ring,
> Amidst these golden glories,
> And fiery stories;
> Whether the sun had been the king.

Besides these main symbols a number of minor images and descriptive passages in *Silex Scintillans* have their obvious counterparts in *Poems* or *Olor Iscanus* : for one instance, lines 25–28 of *The Bird* remind us unmistakably of lines 6–8 in *Upon the Priory Grove*. However, a much more convincing, and compact, demonstration of the essential continuity of Vaughan's poetry can be given from a single early poem, *To the River Isca*.

Here the first passage for notice is the couplet,

> Thus poets—like the nymphs, their pleasing themes—
> Haunted the bubbling springs and gliding streams.

Out of this pagan fancy, christianised and adapted to various Biblical texts, was later to come the picture of Angels, in Old Testament days, seated 'at some fountain's bubbling eye' that Vaughan gives us in the poem *Religion*. Indeed, this transformation is already half accomplished, for in the same descriptive passage, three lines further on, we read :

> Poets—like angels—where they once appear
> Hallow the place.

A much more substantial parallel is to be traced from the description of a poets' Elysium :

> Hence th' ancients say, that from this sickly air
> They pass to regions more refin'd and fair,
> To meadows strew'd with lilies and the rose,
> And shades whose youthful green no old age knows;
> Where all in white they walk, discourse, and sing
> Like bees' soft murmurs, or a chiding spring.

No one can possibly miss the concentration here of words and images that are to form the currency of *Silex Scintillans*— 'sickly air', 'refin'd', 'fair', 'shades', 'youthful green', 'all in white', 'bees', 'chiding spring'. There is also some indication that the poet's ear is haunted, even in unregenerate days, by Biblical phrases, for the line, 'To meadows strew'd with lilies and the rose', sounds very much like an echo from *The Song of Songs* in the Vulgate rendering—'O Rosa Campi! O lilium Convallium',[1] while the phrase, 'all in white', may be a vaguer recol-

---

[1] Quoted by Vaughan as an epigraph to *The British Church*.

lection of something in the New Testament—possibly from Revelation. But, most important of all, this mainly pagan fancy is a clear intimation of Vaughan's later visions of the Christian heaven, of lines like :

> For Thy eternal, living wells
> None stain'd or wither'd shall come near :
> A fresh, immortal green there dwells,
> And spotless white is all the wear.

> *The Seed Growing Secretly*

Another most striking connection with *Silex Scintillans* is to be seen in the lines where Vaughan echoes William Browne's *Britannia's Pastorals* (Book I, Song 2) :

> In all thy journey to the main
> No nitrous clay, nor brimstone-vein
> Mix with thy streams, but may they pass
> Fresh on the air, and clear as glass.

Much more highly elaborated, this image of the polluted, underground stream reappears in *Religion* :

> Religion is a spring,
> That from some secret, golden mine
> Derives her birth. . . .

> But in her long and hidden course,
>   Passing through the Earth's dark veins,
> Grows still from better unto worse,
>   And both her taste and colour stains;

> Then drilling on, learns to increase
>   False echoes and confused sounds,
> And unawares doth often seize
>   On veins of sulphur under ground.

Along with these direct and substantial correspondences there are several smaller resemblances to be noted between *To the River Isca* and various poems in *Silex Scintillans*. For instance, we may observe in lines 39–42 a faint emergence of that association between groves and spiritual experience that we find in

Regeneration[1] and elsewhere. Though metaphors drawn from mercantile activity are never common in Vaughan, we might compare the 'factor-wind', the 'spicy whispers', and the implied reference to the East India trade in lines 62–5 with the 'Eastern traffic' and 'Mountains of spice' in *The Queer*. Again, outside the passages already quoted, there are numerous phrases—'lov'd arbours', 'vocal groves', 'dewy nights', 'sunshine days', 'the turtle's voice'. 'fair days'—which, though they sometimes have general seventeenth-century currency, bear the unmistakable stamp of *Silex Scintillans*. Finally, there are two further sections of the poem that are generally typical of the later Vaughan in language, imagery, and sensibility, even if they cannot be exactly matched with any particular passage (the first has perhaps some kinship with lines 7–8 of 'They are all gone into the world of light') :

[1]
[When] my sun sets, where first it sprang in beams,
I'll leave behind me such a large, kind light,
As shall redeem thee from oblivious night,
And in these vows which—living yet—I pay,
Shed such a previous and enduring ray. . . .

[2]
and whatever Fate
Impose elsewhere, whether the graver state
Or some toy else, may those loud, anxious cares
For dead and dying things—the common wares
And shows of Time—ne'er break thy peace.

There is another certain and most important fact that must be taken into account in any attempt to understand Vaughan's great creative outburst. Besides every poet's dower of imagination, he also possessed (and this is by no means the same gift) a private 'world' of imagination—a world that was limited no doubt, but an individual, coherent, intense, and artistically stimulating one.

[1] See pp. 108–9.

Admittedly, there is only a glimpse of this world in *Poems* and *Olor Iscanus*; but that does not mean that when we speak of it we are merely using a summary metaphor for our total impressions of *Silex Scintillans*. This 'world', which almost certainly originated in those childhood days that Vaughan always looked back to as a time of revelation and rare experience, and which must, from its nature, force, and completeness, have been evolving over many years, is undoubtedly pre-existent to *Silex Scintillans* and in some sense distinct from the poems that embody it. It is the poetry behind the particular poems that so many of us sense whenever we are reading Vaughan's work, a vision and an apprehension of things that is, on the one hand, perfectly reflected through a number of poems that are really one poem, variations on one another, and, on the other hand, is often to be glimpsed only in the gleams and flashes of fragmentary but intensely suggestive lines and phrases. It is distinct, again, from the poems in that it not only forms their substance but is often (sometimes subconsciously) their manifest inspiration and dynamic. It is to be experienced, less vividly and continuously of course, in Vaughan's prose as well as his verse; and its existence explains, as nothing else could, his extraordinary power of assimilating and transmuting, without loss of freshness or originality, his innumerable borrowings from the Bible, Herbert, and other writers.

Definition of this 'world' of Vaughan's imagination—or, if the word is preferred, of his individual vision—will be one of the concerns of several of the ensuing chapters. But some indication of its nature will not be out of place here, partly for introductory reasons and partly to substantiate the proof of its existence.

It is a world (we may say) of continual and marked contrasts, notably of the eternal, primal alternation of day and night, the wonder of daybreak, the mystery and terror of night, with all their rich similars, analogies, and extensions—light and darkness, consciousness and sleep, election and sin, life and death. (This centre of Vaughan's vision can of course be illustrated only by complete poems, *The Morning-Watch* and *The Night* for outstanding examples, but—to mention one small detail—how characteristic it is of him that two lines of meditation on childhood, of an ideal, Eden-like, almost timeless image—

> Fair shining mountains of my pilgrimage
> And flowery vales, whose flow'rs were stars
>> *Looking Back (Thalia Rediviva)*

—are immediately followed by the turn,

> The days and nights of my first happy age.

There is also the perpetual, strange contrast of the near and the far, of the earthly and the otherworldly—primroses and Welsh streams with Scriptural palm-trees and wells, the Brecon landscape with the garden of *The Song of Songs*, the lamps, beds, and cottages of familiar, everyday experience with memories of the 'bright days of Eden' and visions of the 'fresh spicy mornings and eternal beams' of heaven. And, with these, there are again innumerable smaller contrasts—effulgent radiance and eclipse, fructifying dew and blasting frost, vocal streams and stagnant puddles.

A world of contrasting light and darkness, but a world also of candles, lamps, glow-worms, beams and rays, sun and stars, where the streaming light is always predominant and triumphant.

A 'quick world'—one of morning, Spring and Summer, filled continuously with affirmations of life through its intense suggestions of revival and resurrection, youth and freshness, through its constant reminder of seeds, roots, and green growing things hidden under the earth—

> Dear, secret greenness! nurs'd below
> Tempests and winds, and winter-nights

—and through its innumerable images of water in all forms and of flowers and vegetation in bloom and bud—

> Green trees of life, and living streams.

A world—for another unforgettable impression—of strangeness and wonder: where streams run red; where stones, like those 'which in the darkest nights point to their homes', have a sentience and often a mysterious significance; where everything, above and below, is linked by celestial rays and magnetic influences, so that the cock with his grain of star-fire, his 'sunny seed', responds instantly to the return of the sun, and the herbs

> Watch for and know their loving star;

and where all the Creation, birds and beasts, plants, streams, and stones, are perpetually striving towards God, adoring Him, and eagerly expecting the Second Coming.

Finally, subsuming most of these impressions, a world of 'glory'—the 'weaker glories' in the 'gilded Clouds or flowers' of Nature, the 'flowers and shoots of glory' in the soul that is in tune with God, the 'Air of glory' in the walks of heaven—

> So some strange thoughts transcend our wonted themes,
> And into glory peep.

But the core of our question remains. What was the new fire that transmuted those earlier poetic elements that we may still discern in *Silex Scintillans?* What was the compulsion that drove Vaughan to express (and no doubt to deepen, extend, and clarify) that individual vision of his that probably went back to his childhood?

Poor physical health may have had something to do with the miracle, for we have A. E. Housman's testimony, valid perhaps for certain other poets, that 'I have seldom written poetry unless I was rather out of health'.[1] True, the only certain evidence of Vaughan suffering from severe illness—'when I had expected, and had . . . prepared for a message of death'[2]—comes from the period, probably in or about 1653, between the two Parts of *Silex Scintillans*. On the other hand, the onset of this illness, whatever its nature, and the privations experienced during his Civil War service (of which his poem, *Upon a Cloak lent him*, gives us some indication) may have already undermined his

---

[1] *The Name and Nature of Poetry*, p. 49.

[2] The Preface to *Silex Scintillans, Vaughan's Works*, ed. L. C. Martin, p. 392. See also the Introductory Letter to *Flores Solitudinis*, p. 215, and odd lines in the poems of *Silex Scintillans* (Part Two especially) like *Begging II*, ll. 23-4.

health much earlier, in the year or two when he was composing the poems of the first Part of *Silex Scintillans*.

Again, there is the possibility that he had suffered some kind of mental breakdown. Most of his prose translations of this period are obviously relevant to his own needs and condition, and it may not be an accident that two of the four published in 1651 (both entitled *Of the Diseases of the Mind and the Body*) argue the case that mental illness is far worse than physical.

Admittedly, these speculations about his state of health are guesswork. But if we are ignorant about many important details of his life in the late 1640's, there is much that we do know for certain. As a young man, in his middle twenties, he had fought for a short time in the Civil War;[1] and *Silex Scintillans* reveals plainly that this experience had left him with a deep horror of bloodshed. Being on the losing side, he had not only to endure, for an indefinite period, the suppression of those religious and political ideals he had fought for, but also to abandon his ambitious early dreams of some dazzling career in London :

> O Thou who didst deny to me
> This world's ador'd felicity,
> And ev'ry big imperious lust,
> Which fools admire in sinful dust.
>
> *The Request (Thalia Rediviva)*

He was back—in all probability for good—in the remote countryside of his boyhood, back to an obscure, private, restricted life of straitened means. In this same period the personal experience of death had pressed upon him with exceptional heaviness—during the war with the loss of his friends R.W. and Mr R. Hall, and afterwards with the passing of his much loved younger brother William in 1648 and of his first wife sometime between the publication of the two Parts of *Silex Scintillans*. Also in the late 1640's he became closely acquainted with the work of George Herbert, and was deeply impressed by both Herbert's poetry and life. At the same time he was prob-

---

[1] If the poems ever left any doubt on this matter, F. E. Hutchinson in his *Henry Vaughan* has conclusively shown that the poet took an active part in the fighting of the Civil War.

ably infected, more seriously than ever before, by his twin brother's passionate enthusiasm for hermetic philosophy. Finally, and most importantly of all, after passing through a period in which he endeavoured to sustain himself with stoic philosophy, he underwent a most profound and intense Christian 'regeneration'.

These biographical facts enable us to understand something at least of the mystery of his sudden poetic flowering.

To say the simplest—though perhaps not the least important —thing first, they reveal that the period in which he wrote *Silex Scintillans* was almost certainly one of great intellectual, emotional, and spiritual crisis—of tension, pressure, and conflict. He was threatened with spiritual (and perhaps, as I have suggested, physical) collapse. He slowly re-made himself—into a resigned, devout Christian of deep, assured convictions, and also we may add, for there is nothing grotesque in this conjunction of the spiritual and physical, into a vigorous, hardworking man who lived to a considerable age. There had never been anything comparable with this upheaval in his life before; there never was again.

Certainly innumerable men have passed through the same kind of psychological and spiritual turmoil without writing a single line of verse, let alone a lyrical masterpiece like *The Morning-Watch* or *The Night*. But Vaughan was a man of rich imaginative resources, well practised in verse composition, deeply, widely, and curiously read—one who might have said with Wordsworth

> for I neither seem
> To lack that first great gift, the vital soul. . . .
> Nor am I naked of external things,
> Forms, images, nor numerous other aids
> Of less regard, though won perhaps with toil.[1]

It is therefore not unreasonable to see in all this emotional and intellectual ferment a compulsive force that would both drive him to poetry and at the same time fire and integrate his writing

[1] Bk. I, 149–56.

with that urgency and purpose that had been so completely lacking in the merely accomplished exercises of *Poems* and *Olor Iscanus*. Possibly Vaughan glimpsed his own creative condition when he wrote:

> Poor birds sing best, and prettiest show,
> When their nest is fall'n and broken.
>
> *Begging II*

The above quotation from *The Prelude* is particularly relevant in that a surprisingly close and convincing parallel can be drawn between Vaughan's situation and Wordsworth's, when the latter leapt, even more miraculously, from the versifying of his *Evening Walk and Descriptive Sketches* (these, like the pieces in *Poems* and *Olor Iscanus*, highly derivative) to the *Lyrical Ballads* and into his great creative period. Parallel with the defeat of the Royalist cause, and all that this meant for Vaughan, we may set Wordsworth's shattering disillusionment at the outcome of the French Revolution. Like Vaughan (as we may reasonably surmise of him), Wordsworth went through a desperate period of intellectual and spiritual crisis, which is recorded in the last books of *The Prelude*. Both poets, though under different compulsions, returned from the world of affairs into the countryside of their childhood; and where Vaughan found his salvation in a Christian faith that significantly embraced Nature, Wordsworth discovered his in a much vaguer, though equally profound, religion of Nature. Both poets—Wordsworth of course much more than Vaughan—found great solace, relevance, and inspiration in their recollections of childhood. Both were given direction and most fruitfully stimulated by the influence of another writer—Vaughan by Herbert and Wordsworth by Coleridge. Further, though this parallel is admittedly a slight one, the emotional effect of Vaughan's loss of his brother William may to some extent be compared with that of Wordsworth's 'loss' of Annette.

There is not the slightest reason to doubt that Vaughan had always been a nominal Christian. It is possible also that the

shock of historic crisis, compelling choice, brought deep convictions to the surface, that he joined the Royalist army because
(among other motives) he was ready to sacrifice his life for the
cause of the Anglican Church. But apart from this possibility—
and it is no more than that—there is nothing in his early life or
in the poetry he wrote up to 1648 to suggest that he took religion
at all seriously. On the contrary, even if, in the familiar way of
the reformed, he later exaggerated his 'sinful youth', he was
clearly a gay, convivial young fellow,[1] hoping for a successful
worldly career and enjoying the pleasures of life with a pagan
sensuous gusto that is often remarkably like that of the young
Keats[2] of *Endymion*:

> A bed of roses I'll provide for thee,
> And crystal springs shall drop thee melody.
> The breathing shades we'll haunt, where ev'ry leaf
> Shall whisper us asleep, though thou art deaf.
> Those waggish nymphs, too, which none ever yet
> Durst make love to, we'll teach the loving fit;
> We'll suck the coral of their lips, and feed
> Upon their spicy breath, a meal at need;
> Rove in their amber-tresses. . . .

In Amicum Foeneratorem

We have his own word for it that he had definitely resisted any
call to a serious religious life,[3] while as late as 1647 (possibly
later) we find him writing about his friend's failure to visit him
in the flippant vein of:

[1] The diffident, moping-melancholy, retiring, humourless youth that Miss
Helen Ashton pictured in her fictional life of Vaughan, *The Swan of Usk*, could
never have written *To My Ingenuous Friend, R.W., A Rhapsodis*, with all its robust,
convivial spirit, *In Amicum Foeneratorem, To His Friend*—and *Upon a Cloke Lent
him by Mr J. Ridsley*.

[2] Conviviality and friendship, literary enthusiasm for certain 'bards', fondness for
the cup, Elysian dreamings, enchantment with the Endymion story—all these
themes (and often the treatment of them) create a surprising bond between the
young Vaughan and the Keats of the *Epistles*, parts of *Sleep and Poetry*, 'Bards of
Passion', and *Lines on the Mermaid Tavern*. To the passage quoted in the text from
In Amicum Foeneratorem we might add *To My Ingenuous Friend, R.W.*, ll. 29–36,
and *A Rhapsodis*, ll. 64–70. *To Lysimachus* is another poem that is filled with a
Keatsian sensuousness.

[3] See the first Dedication poem, ll. 9–12, and *To the Holy Bible*, ll. 17–22.

Or is't thy piety? for who can tell
But thou may'st prove devout, and love a cell,
And—like a badger—with attentive looks
In the dark hole sit rooting up of books.
Quick hermit! what a peaceful change hadst thou,
Without the noise of haircloth, whip, or vow!

To His Retired Friend

From about 1649 (assuming that the composition of the first Part of *Silex Scintillans* occupied at least a year) to 1654 he turned his poetic attention entirely to religious verse, and these years were also the period of his devotional prose works, *The Mount of Olives* and *Flores Solitudinis*. To say nothing of the Preface to *Silex Scintillans* (including its address to 'all penitent and reformed Spirits') and nothing of certain of the poems like *Distraction*, *The Relapse*, *Idle Verse*, the first part of *Retirement*, *Mount of Olives II*, *The Garland* and 'Fair and Young Light' that speak directly of a reclamation from ungodliness to positive belief, all Vaughan's writing of this time reveals a man whose life has been completely transformed and is now entirely centred in the Christian religion. While there are no grounds for thinking that he ever experienced any sudden, dramatic Pauline 'conversion', he certainly underwent a decisive spiritual regeneration, which covered the period of *Silex Scintillans* and probably began in 1648, since there is the plainest evidence, in 'Thou that knowst for whom I mourn' and elsewhere, that the untimely death of his younger brother in that year first set him seriously thinking about his spiritual state :

But 'twas my sin that forc'd Thy hand
To cull this primrose out,
That by Thy early choice forewarn'd
My soul might look about.

There would be no call for repeating these well-known and clear-pointing facts were it not that in recent years some doubt has been cast on the reality of Vaughan's regeneration, notably in Professor Kermode's essay, 'The Private Imagery of Henry Vaughan'.[1] Besides expressing the strongest scepticism about

[1] *R.E.S.*, vol. i, no. 3, July 1950, pp. 206–25.

the regeneration, this study attempted to upturn accepted views by maintaining that the inspiration of *Silex Scintillans* was predominantly a literary one, that 'the conversion rather a poetic than a religious experience'.

It is impossible in a limited space to deal adequately with Professor Kermode's argument, which implicitly raises the whole complex question of the relationship between life and literature and appears to deny the validity of 'religious' (or for that matter 'love' or any other life-related) poetry altogether. His essay is most valuable in stressing, with some acute analysis, the importance of Vaughan's purely literary inspiration; and no one can disagree with him when he reminds us of the 'absolute uselessness of attempts to discuss the poetry as if its value were determined by [Vaughan's] religious life'. But his denial that the poetry was centrally inspired by that religious life is flatly contradicted by Vaughan himself, who, in his Preface to *Silex Scintillans*, expresses the hope that the book will be 'as useful now in the public, as it hath been to me in private'.[1] That the poet was not deceiving himself in thinking that his work was rooted in his devotional life is surely proved by the fact that many of his poems are unquestionably reflections on some Biblical text, by the strong possibility, as L. L. Martz has suggested,[2] that a number of them were based on a precise contemporary mode of meditation, and by the essential relationship between *Silex Scintillans* and his book of devotional practice, *The Mount of Olives*.

This relationship is not to be dismissed by Professor Kermode's passing acknowledgement that *The Mount of Olives* occasionally gives us the prose-content of a particular poem: the kinship is a continuous one of word, image, and sensibility as

---

[1] *Works*, p. 392.

[2] *The Poetry of Meditation, passim*. See particularly the discussion of 'I walkt the other day', pp. 64–7, *The Search*, pp. 86–90, and *Vanity of Spirit*, pp. 150–2. The mode of meditation referred to in the text is described by Martz as 'falling into three distinguishable portions, corresponding to the acts of memory, understanding, and will—portions which we might call composition, analysis, and colloquy (p. 38).

17

well as of idea and sentiment, and the antithesis between prose and poetry is invalid, since the writing in *The Mount of Olives* is often truly poetic. Again, his assertion that 'it is very doubtful that Vaughan's poetry is any more closely related to his religious experience than Sidney's *Astrophel and Stella* is to his amorous experience' is entirely misleading and irrelevant: the sonnets were largely a product of 'feigning' (as Sidney would have understood the word); Vaughan's deliberate aim, on the contrary, was 'true unfeigned verse' 'flowing from a true, practick piety'.[1]

But all these arguments must be inevitably limited in their effect. Primarily our convictions about the nature of Vaughan's inspiration will depend on what we get from the poems; and if Professor Kermode really considers that *The Night*, for instance, is principally the working out of a major image-complex and not also the expression of some of Vaughan's deepest devotional feelings in the night hours, always for him a time of peculiar and momentous experience, it is unlikely that he will ever be reasoned out of a one-sided (if highly sensitive) response to that lyric.

If we accept the reality and depth of Vaughan's regeneration, in what respects may it be said to have inspired and shaped his poetry?

For one, it gave him something that had been notably lacking in his earlier writing, a vital and engrossing subject. No need to stress that important subjects, and the writer's attitude to them, do not necessarily produce important poetry—often the opposite; but, attracting and patterning the poet's experience towards a magnetic centre, infusing him with seriousness, passion, and urgency, they certainly create some of the indispensable conditions for important poetry. For the first time in his life Vaughan really had something to say for himself as a poet.

[1] The first quoted phrase is from *Anguish*, l. 15, the second from the Preface to *Silex Scintillans*, *Works*, p. 391.

Next, one surmises, with some degree of certainty, that it was the urge to communicate his religious experience that at last threw fully open and brought into poetry all the rich world of his private imagination. Particularly because of those qualities of contrast and antithesis that we have already noticed, this world was one peculiarly suited to the expression of the great Christian opposites, while much of its substance—mornings, waters, green things below the earth (all objects of sensibility in the first place)—were readily translatable into spiritual metaphor and symbol. On the other hand, religion was not simply the magic key that unlocked this world; it also enriched it and to some extent ordered it into coherence, transforming its images, which were sometimes conventional and undistinguished, into complex, compelling symbols. The stars and streams of *Silex Scintillans* are the stars and streams of *Poems* and *Olor Iscanus*; but they are something else too, and it is the fire of Vaughan's regeneration that has transmuted them.

Again, we can certainly trace a number of religious ideas in *Silex Scintillans* that are important and notable either because they are recurrent or because they sometimes inspired whole poems. One such, derived largely no doubt from Vaughan's hermetic reading, was his deep and imaginative conception of the Divine immanence in Nature and hence of the religious significance of all the workings of Nature.[1] Another was his continual thought of the Fall, both as an historical event, in which Nature as well as man was corrupted, and as an experience repeated in the life of each individual. This led him to the doctrine of predestination, with its rigid distinction between the elect and the non-elect, and to a belief in the inevitable decay of religious feeling; but these conclusions were counterbalanced—and perhaps

---

[1] Cf. H. C. White, *The Metaphysical Poets*, p. 290: 'That God was everywhere was a position to which all Christians would have agreed, as they would have agreed that the whole universe and its creatures was the work of His hands. But in their preoccupations with the central issues of justice and mercy, of power and satisfaction, they were on the whole not disposed to emphasise, still less to do justice to, the implications of the Christian doctrine of the immanence of God in the world of His creation.'

contradicted[1]—partly by his dream of 'the primitive Angelic life' of man and partly by his idealisation, based on the text of Matthew 18. 3, of the innocence, purity, and vision of childhood, of the Eden momentarily regained :

> Dear, harmless age! the short, swift span
> Where weeping Virtue parts with man;
> Where love without lust dwells, and bends
> What way we please without self-ends.
>
> An age of mysteries! which he
> Must live twice that would God's face see;
> Which angels guard, and with it play,
> Angels! which foul men drive away.

Childhood

Everywhere Christ was the centre of his religious thought, and, like most religious writers of his age, he regarded him above all else as the Mediator, the God become man, who has redeemed humanity from its fallen state. Hence his poetry throws a heavy stress on the Incarnation and Passion, the offer of redemptive grace, and the significance of the Holy Communion, the latter forming the subject of several poems. He shows little awareness—in his poetry at any rate—of the humanity of Christ, nor is he ever, like Herbert, inspired by a sense of intimate, personal relationship with Him.

Perhaps because he wrote as one of the regenerate, he held the strongest convictions about the perversity, blindness,[2] and instability of the 'mule, unruly Man'—himself notably included :

[1] W. Lewis Bettany writes, in the Introduction to his edition of *Silex Scintillans* (p. xxxi) : 'the poet seems so enamoured of this theory of the original spotlessness of the soul, that in *Childhood* he calmly repudiates the orthodox Christian doctrine of original sin, and, in a beautiful fallacy, transfers to the childhood of the individual man that innocence which elsewhere he has predicated of the childhood of the race, clenching his argument by a description of infancy as an age "which he must live twice that would God's face see".'

[2] H. C. White, *op. cit.*, p. 297, observes : 'In common with the German mystics Vaughan found the saddest consequences of the Fall in the blindness and the deadness of the spirit in man.'

The world
Is full of voices; man is call'd, and hurl'd
By each; he answers all,
Knows ev'ry note and call;
Hence, still
Fresh dotage tempts, or old usurps his will.

Distraction

From this attitude to mankind comes an emphatic and persistent affirmation in his poetry of the spiritual value of affliction, and while he gratefully accepts the humanising of religion that was brought about by the Incarnation, he still welcomes (as we may see in *The Law and the Gospel*, for example) the stern authoritarianism and spirit of fear embodied in so much of the Old Testament.

Ideas of this sort give the poems of *Silex Scintillans* some intellectual weight and also serve at times to brace them structurally, so that they are never mere visionary raptures or emotional outpourings. But, when we have allowed for some individuality of stress and an original regard for Nature, his ideas remain on the whole commonplace and orthodox; they lack any depth or complexity, apart from an occasional reinforcement from hermetic notions; and above all, as they are never the predominant inspiration of his finest poems, so they are often the main inspiration of his weakest ones. Further, whatever may have been the intellectual inclination of his hermetic studies or of his later interest in Natural History, his religious poetry reveals no special gift for spiritual analysis and no particular bent towards speculation, inquiry, or argument. Indeed, in Part Two of *Silex Scintillans*, we may detect a deliberate turning away from the burden of thought about religion to simple, even child-like, affirmations of faith:

Those observations are but foul,
Which make me wise to lose my soul.   *Childhood*

What chiefly inspired his religious poetry (quantitatively, and in his greatest lyrics) was the emotional experience of his regeneration and devotion—his tensions, anxieties, frustrations and moments of assurance, his defeats and triumphs, his eager, though never feverish, spirit of yearning and questing towards God; and though the ideas and beliefs on which he meditated no doubt pressed for their images and symbols, it was probably these emotional states, rather than the ideas, that evoked and fused with that world of imagination which was the other primary source of his poetry.

Out of his intense and complex emotional experience we may distinguish three notes that are pervasive throughout *Silex Scintillans* and memorably concentrated in its masterpieces.

First, there is his most moving expression of spiritual exile, estrangement, and severance from God; and though Miss Holmes is probably right in her opinion that he never experienced the 'terror of alienation'[1] that Herbert, Donne, and Bunyan suffered in their various ways, no other English poet of the seventeenth century communicates with greater poignancy the anguish of separation and spiritual homesickness :

> My dew, my dew! my early love,
> My soul's bright food, Thy absence kills!
> Hover not long, eternal Dove!
> Life without Thee is loose, and spills.
>
> *The Seed Growing Secretly*

Secondly, contrasting with this note but complementing it, there is the vibrant exhilaration he sometimes conveys through such lyrics as *The Morning-Watch*, *The Night* and *Unprofitableness* of moments of visitation and divine presence—a singularly rich and convincing impression of refreshment, revival, and burgeoning, which broadens (inevitably as it seems) into all the wonders of morning, youth, and resurrection. And, inseparable from this, there is always an ultimate joyousness in his poetry springing from his assured and tested conviction that true joy is attainable, even perhaps momentarily in our mortal life.

Thirdly, a result both of the visionary, dreaming side of his experience and of that part of his imaginative world that embodies it—his glimpses, for example, of the quiet, tranquillity, and ineffable radiance of heaven—his poetry often evokes a

---

[1] *Elizabeth Holmes, Henry Vaughan and the Hermetic Philosophy*, p.51

strange otherworldliness that marks it off from all the other religious verse of his age.

But this 'otherworldliness' certainly does not spell 'mysticism'. Admittedly, there are some elements in his poetry that belong to that common field of spiritual endeavour lying between the purgative (and to some extent the illuminative) stages of mysticism and the more familiar religious disciplines of devotion and meditation; and, without unduly confusing matters, we may perhaps describe these elements as 'mystical'. Again, there may be something in *Silex Scintillans* of what Miss H. C. White has termed the 'emotional ground-work' of mysticism—'a vague sense of the incompleteness of the immediately present', 'a sense of the environing mystery of the universe'—though, as she herself admitted, these tenuous and fugitive sentiments amount to no more than 'the sort of feeling that will make a man walk the ways of the world in wonder and delight rather than the passion that makes the mystic forsake all to concentrate on the spiritual labour of the mystic way'.[1] But so far as the essential ecstatic experiences of mysticism are concerned—the transcendance or extinction of self, the apprehension of an order of reality beyond and entirely different from our human, earthly reality, the merging into the divine spirit that is this transcendental reality, and the unique focusing, peace and fulfilment of spirit that is the consummation of these experiences—Vaughan has little or nothing to say about them in his poetry, nor does he ever claim to have known them.[2]

---

[1] *Op. cit.*, pp. 305–6. See also the remark (p. 308): 'There is something other worldly about Vaughan's visions that on the whole is not to be found in either Herbert or Crashaw. That is the secret, I think, of that "mystical feeling" that is so common an impression of Vaughan's works.'

[2] The most sustained argument for Vaughan's mysticism is to be found in Itrat-Husain's *The Mystical Element in the Metaphysical Poets of the Seventeenth Century*. But Itrat-Husain's industrious compilation of the alleged 'mystical' utterances of Vaughan—innumerable isolated lines rather than entire poems—never adds up to the conclusion he is obviously seeking. What emerges from his exhaustive analysis is a predominantly devotional poet of visionary moments, not a mystic; and he is himself forced to admit that 'there is no evidence in Vaughan's poems of his ever having experienced the higher stages of mystical life, the "dark night" of the soul, or the union with God' (pp. 231–2).

Finally, another most important clue to the secret of Vaughan's realisation of himself as a poet is to be found in Dowden's remark that his 'best and most characteristic work came from a region below his conscious intelligence'.[1] To borrow a phrase of Auden's, though from a different context, the poet who wrote *Silex Scintillans* was undoubtedly one 'fed by the involuntary powers', a poet suddenly enabled to draw on all the rich, spontaneous workings of his subconscious imagination.

This new mode of inspiration, which Dowden perceived without apparently understanding very much, seems to have taken two main forms. In the first place (as will be shown in the later studies of some particular poems) many of his lyrics, including most of the best ones, evolve not so much through the logical connected development from thought to thought as by way of association, sometimes rather oblique in nature, and by the spontaneous proliferating of some unifying complex of imagery. In his earlier poems, on the other hand, which belong to the central metaphysical tradition, his writing had been much more consciously organised, much more dependent on logical and argumentative forms of structure.

Secondly, *Silex Scintillans* is quite remarkable for the way in which its numerous recurrent image-clusters, besides inspiring so many poems, come together without the writer's conscious ordering. Time and again one constituent of a compound image will call up the rest of it through what can only have been some process of subconscious association.

The most outstanding example of this process is to be found in the blood–water–spirit complex, which, because of its Biblical origin, has been held over to the next chapter. But there are some other examples that are hardly less striking, like that of the cloud-star image.

On a number of occasions, as in the last part of *The Morning-Watch*, this image is employed as a controlled, unified whole, usually symbolising deprivation or frustration. But there are at least eight occasions in Vaughan's poetry where 'stars' and

[1] *Puritan and Anglican*, p. 121.

'clouds' occur together without any logical compulsion, and it will be noticed that the association is a curiously persistent one, since example 2 comes from an early poem, while 3–8 cover both Parts of *Silex Scintillans*:

[1]

Th' hast clear'd the prospect to our harmless hill,
Of late years clouded with imputed ill,
And the soft, youthful couples there may move,
As chaste as stars converse and smile above.

To Sir William D'avenant

[2]

Like twinkling stars her eyes invite
All gazers to so sweet a light,
But then two archèd clouds of brown
Stand o'er, and guard them with a frown.

Fida

[3]

To put on clouds instead of light,
    And clothe the morning-star with dust. . . .

The Incarnation and Passion

[4]

Stars now vanish without number,
Sleepy planets set and slumber,
The pursy clouds disband and scatter,
All except some sudden matter,
Not one beam triumphs, but from far
    That morning-star.

The Dawning

[5]

It glows and glitters in my cloudy breast,
    Like stars upon some gloomy grove.

'They are all gone into the world of light'

[6]

Did some cloud,
Fix'd to a tent, descend and shroud
My distress'd Lord? or did a star,
Beckon'd by Thee. . . .

The Dwelling-Place

25

[7]

At length my life's kind angel came,
   And with his bright and busy wing
Scatt'ring that cloud show'd me the flame,
   Which straight like morning-stars did sing.

The Agreement

[8]

And clouds but cool his dog-star days.

Affliction (Thalia Rediviva)

Apart from these obvious examples of a subconscious association in Vaughan's mind of clouds and stars, there are several
other passages where the same association is probably at work,
though in a less immediately apparent way. One such is the following extract from *Rules and Lessons*, in which (to judge by
other poems) 'thickest night' is almost synonymous with
'clouds' :

God pries
Through thickest nights; though then the sun be far
Do thou the works of day, and rise a star.

Again, because 'eclipse' in Vaughan's poetry more frequently
refers to the intermission of starlight than the obscuring of sun
or moon, we probably have another latent example of this
association in the lines :

Condemning thoughts—like sad eclipses—scowl
   Upon his soul,
And clouds of crying witnesses without
   Pursued him with one shout.

The World

Another most interesting image, for our present theme, is the
complex : bed–bed-curtains–grave–death. Twice this image
is used by Vaughan as an organised unity. In *Death: A Dialogue*,
where the Body is contemplating its interment, we have the
lines :

I'll wish my curtains off, to free
Me from so dark and sad a bed.

This corresponds with the conclusion of *The Morning-Watch* :

> So in my bed,
> That curtain'd grave. . . .

But the constituents of this complex sometimes come together through an involuntary association, and we have an example of this process in one of Vaughan's earliest poems—in the purely decorative lines in *Les Amours* where the disconsolate lover is picturing his destined grave :

> O'er all the tomb a sudden spring
> Of crimson flowers, whose drooping heads
> Shall curtain o'er their mournful beds. . . .

In this passage it is almost certainly 'tomb' that has generated the full complex, not so much because it comes first, but because it is necessary, and inevitable, in the argument of the poem. This 'tomb' has probably suggested the incidental detail of 'beds' for the flowers (earlier in the poem the lover's grave has been familiarly described as a 'cold bed'), and Vaughan's fixed image of the particular bed of his own time[1] has brought with it the unexpected verb 'curtain'.

There are three probable instances of this same subconscious association in *Silex Scintillans*. The first occurs in *Rules and Lessons*, where, following a stanza on death, which contains the word 'grave' and concludes with the lines,

> but the good man lies
> Entombèd many days before he dies,

Vaughan goes on to speak of bed-time in the image of

> close not thy eyes
> Up with thy curtains.

(Shortly after this 'curtains' we again find 'die' and 'dead age'.) In the next poem, *Corruption*, while his automatic *cloud-shroud* rhyme may have had much to do with one of the transitions, it is fairly likely that the association we are considering also helped

---

[1] There are three simple subconscious associations between bed and curtains— *To the best, and most accomplished Couple*, ll. 11–12; Boethius, *Lib. 2, Metrum 3*, ll. 1–3; and *Looking Back*, l. 7.

to determine the movement from the metaphor of the drawn 'curtains' (signifying God's present obscurity) to a description of a fallen, corrupted world that is strongly associated with death :

> I see, Thy curtains are close-drawn; Thy bow
> Looks dim too in the cloud;
> Sin triumphs still, and man is sunk below
> The centre, and his shroud.

The third example, from stanza 5 of 'I walk't the other day', is perhaps a rather less convincing one. But it seems very possible that the explicit emergence in this stanza of the theme of death and his dead brother had some influence on the way Vaughan describes his action of reburying the plant that he had dug up for scrutiny :

> I threw the clothes quite o'er his head;
> And stung with fear
> Of my own frailty, dropp'd down many a tear
> Upon his bed.

In addition to these, there are a number of image-patterns where the combination appears to be always of an associational kind. One striking example is: scents (and/or flowers)–sun–divine visitation. This is to be first found, without any religious significance, in one of the pre-*Silex Scintillans* poems :

> The careless ranks of flowers that spread
> Their perfum'd bosoms to his head,
> And with an open, free embrace,
> Did entertain his beamy face.
>
> *To Amoret Gone From Him*

There are three obvious instances of this complex in *Silex Scintillans* :

> [1]
> The unthrift Sun shot vital gold. . . .
> The air was all in spice
> And every bush
> A garland wore.
>
> *Regeneration*

[2]

So from Lahai-roi's well, some spicy cloud,
Woo'd by the sun, swells up to be his shroud,
And from her moist womb weeps a fragrant shower,
Which, scatter'd in a thousand pearls, each flower
And herb partakes.

Isaac's Marriage

[3]

I flourish, and once more
Breathe all perfumes and spice;
I smell a dew like myrrh, and all the day
Wear in my bosom a full Sun.

Unprofitableness

The opening of *Mount of Olives II* gives us a fourth example:
here, admittedly, the image of God as the sun is implicit,[1] but
the pattern is unquestionably the one we are considering:

When first I saw True Beauty, and Thy joys
Active as light, and calm without all noise,
Shin'd on my soul, I felt through all my pow'rs
Such a rich air of sweets, as evening show'rs,
Fann'd by a gentle gale convey, and breathe
On some parch'd bank, crown'd with a flow'ry wreath.

Another example of this kind of associational linkage is the
combination of 'healing wings' with sun, an association originat-
ing in Malachi 4. 2: 'But unto you that fear my name shall the
Sun of righteousness arise with healing in his wings.' There are
two clear examples of this in *Silex Scintillans*:

[1]

Thy long expected healing wings could see
When Thou didst rise!
And, what can never more be done,
Did at midnight speak with the Sun!

The Night

[2]

Thy lines are rays the true Sun sheds;
Thy leaves are healing wings He spreads.

The Agreement

[1] With the three previous examples in the text, the idea of divine visitation or
communion is to be found in their general context.

The poem *The Jews* affords another probable, if not certain, example of this combination, for the two lines that fuse the 'healing wings' and 'Sun of righteousness' of Malachi—

> Did sadly note His healing rays
> Would shine elsewhere—

are shortly afterwards followed, in a fresh development of ideas, by the image,

> And the same Sun, which here declines
> And sets, etc.

Smaller instances of the same phenomenon are to be observed fairly frequently. One is the half a dozen or more conjunctions of 'shades' or 'groves' with 'springs' or 'wells', and here it is particularly interesting to notice that one of Vaughan's interpolations in his translation of Ovid, *De Ponto*, Lib. 3, reads:

> with many fancied springs
> And groves.

Another example is the pattern (breaking) bud–dew–blood:

[1]
> Some drops of Thy all-quick'ning blood
> Fell on my heart; those made it bud,
> And put forth thus. . . .

Dedication Poem I

[2]
> with what flowers
> And shoots of glory, my soul breaks and buds. . . .
> This dew fell on my breast;
> O how it bloods. . . .

The Morning-Watch

[3]
> I threaten heaven, and from my cell
> Of clay and frailty break and bud,
> Touch'd by Thy fire and breath; Thy blood,
> Too is my dew, and springing well.

Disorder and Frailty

All this rich and varied nourishment from the 'involuntary powers', which, as we shall see, also affected his borrowings from Herbert and, to a lesser extent, from the Bible, may do little to explain the quality of Vaughan's achievement in *Silex Scintillans*. But it is a fair surmise that this kind of inspiration had much to do with the fertility and fluency of his six productive years, a period when it can be said of him that he is often a poet like the Coleridge of *The Ancient Mariner* and *Kubla Khan*, one who

> on honey-dew hath fed,
> And drunk the milk of Paradise.

CHAPTER II

THE BIBLE

No book of seventeenth-century poetry bears more obvious signs of the impress of the Authorized Version of the Bible than *Silex Scintillans*.

To begin with, there are at least twenty poems in the two Parts—something like a sixth of the book, that is to say—that are mainly inspired by Biblical personages, incidents, and texts (these texts mainly of a doctrinal sort). Further, with about a third of these poems, chiefly the ones based on some text, 'inspired' can be used in a very literal sense, for in all probability they are the outcome of spiritual exercise such as L. L. Martz describes in *The Poetry of Meditation*—not so much because they follow the order of composition, analysis, and colloquy, though some of them do, as because they read like intent cogitations on some Scriptural incident or text that Vaughan felt to be of particular significance. In this group we might include *Isaac's Marriage*, 'And do they so?'—and probably *Death I* and *Man's Fall and Recovery*—in Part I, and *Ascension Day*, *Trinity Sunday*, *Jesus Weeping I*, *The Rainbow*, *The Men of War*, and *Jacob's Pillow and Pillar* in Part II. At all events, 'meditations' or not, these poems are to be clearly distinguished from those in which an accompanying Biblical text merely provides some relevant quotation.

Again, the picture of Nature that emerges from *Silex Scintillans* is intensely and continually coloured with Biblical reminiscences. Time and again Vaughan leaves the impression that he is looking up at the Breconshire landscape, its hills and valleys, its trees and streams, straight from the pages of the Bible, with haunting visions of Eden and of the pastoral life of Abraham and the patriarchs still glimmering before his eyes.

Indeed, the first *Mount of Olives* poem almost amounts to a manifesto for this kind of descriptive writing. The landscape he depicts, through this Old Testament veil, is much like Bunyan's in several of his descriptive passages and even more like Samuel Palmer's pastoral studies (these also star-lit and rich in water and trees) of the 'Shoreham' period.[1] There is a singularly beautiful example of such writing, fresh with all Vaughan's 'Eden' quality, at the beginning of *The Rainbow*:

> Still young and fine! and what is still in view
> We slight as old and soil'd, though fresh and new.
> How bright wert thou, when Shem's admiring eye
> Thy burnish'd, flaming arch did first descry!
> When Terah, Nahor, Haran, Abram, Lot,
> The youthful world's grey fathers in one knot,
> Did with intentive looks watch every hour
> For thy new light, and trembled at each shower!
> When thou dost shine, Darkness looks white and fair,
> Storms turn to music, clouds to smiles and air:
> Rain gently spends his honey-drops, and pours
> Balm on the cleft earth, milk on grass and flowers.
> Bright pledge of peace and sunshine!

Here, even when Vaughan turns away from his direct reference to the world's first rainbow, Scriptural associations remain strong—in the figurative use of 'milk' and 'honey', and perhaps in 'balm', though this last word also has hermetic connections. This feature is worth noticing because, although there are only a few passages as markedly Biblical as this one, many of his descriptions contain some odd word or phrase that reminds us of the Old Testament. His springs are commonly Jacob's Well or streams of living waters; his trees oaks and junipers beneath which angels converse with men, or (conspicuously) palms; his hills the mountains of spices of *The Song of Songs*, that favourite Biblical book that colours so much of his descriptive writing.

As one would expect, his attitude to Nature owes very much less to the Bible. But there are moments when he suggests some-

---

[1] Miss Mahood, *Poetry and Humanism*, p. 255, has already made this comparison with Samuel Palmer.

thing of the spirit of the Psalmist, while one text—*Etenim res Creatae exerto Capite observantes expectant revelationem Filiorum Dei* (Rom. 8. 19)—must have run continuously in his mind whenever he was writing of Nature and the creatures.

Besides these Biblical themes and subjects, Vaughan's poems are filled with Scriptural allusions. Proof of his wide and close reading of the Bible, these references differ a good deal in their accessibility to the modern reader. Anyone who has ever read Genesis will take without difficulty the reference[1] in the first stanza of *Providence* to the Angel who

> show'd that holy well,
> Which freed poor Hagar from her fears
> And turn'd to smiles the begging tears
> Of young, distressèd Ishmael.

But even the reader who knows Genesis well may miss the allusion in *Begging II*—

> Well fare those blessed days of old,
> When Thou didst hear the *weeping lad!*[2]

—which refers to the same episode, not to Vaughan's own youth, or the other Ishmael reference in *The Timber* (ll. 47–8). Again, while everyone will at once recognise the allusion in *The Pursuit* (ll. 9–12) to the story of the Prodigal Son, fewer are likely to connect the 'white winged Reapers' in the beautiful last line of *The Seed Growing Secretly* with the parable of the tares (Matt. 13. 36–43).[3]

Usually these allusions serve as quite straightforward illustrations, and there is rarely anything very surprising in Vaughan's treatment of them, for he held the text of the Bible in sacred respect, condemning those writers who had been 'so irreverently bold as to dash Scriptures and the sacred Relations of God with their impious conceits' (Preface to *Silex Scintillans*).

[1] Genesis 16. 7.
[2] Vaughan's italics indicate that this is an allusion.
[3] See especially v. 39: 'the harvest is the end of the world; and the reapers are the angels.'

Occasionally, however, he does delight us with some bold and original turn, as for instance in his treatment of the 'swordlike gleam'[1] at the end of 'Joy of my life', his forceful, compressed, and very metaphysical conclusion to the argument of *Man's Fall and Recovery*—

> so made
> Of their Red Sea, a spring; I wash, they wade

—and in his image of the Bible, with its effective pun, as

> healing leaves,
> Blown from the tree of life to us
> By His breath whom my dead heart heaves.
> *The Agreement*

Slight adaptations of an allusion, though not numerous, are a little more common. A typical example of this kind may be found in the first of the Dedication poems:

> Indeed I had some here to hire
> Which long resisted Thy desire,
> That ston'd Thy servants, and did move
> To have Thee murder'd for Thy love.

This is plainly an allusion to the parable of the wicked husband-men (Matt. 21. 33–41), but whereas Christ was speaking chiefly of men's persecution of God's prophets, himself included, Vaughan is talking about those forces in his own heart that once resisted the proffer of Divine grace. In *The Timber* (ll. 47–8) he gives a similar personal twist to his Ishmael reference.

Particularly prominent among his allusions are those to various 'stones'—the corner-stone of Christ in *The Search* (l. 48), the Judaic Tables of the Law in *Man's Fall and Recovery* (l. 23) and *The Stone* (l. 49), and the 'white stone' of Revelation 2. 17 in *Rules and Lessons* (l. 28). Where, in the first *Jesus Weeping* poem, he writes,

> Had not the babes 'Hosanna' cried,
> The stones had spoke what you denied,

he is doubtless alluding to Christ's words, '. . . I tell you that, if

[1] See Genesis 3. 24.

these should hold their peace, the stones would immediately cry out' (Luke 19. 40); and in *The Stone*, in the lines,

> stones,
> Which some think dead, shall all at once
> With one attesting voice detect
> Those secret sins we least suspect,

he is certainly thinking, as his epigraph indicates, of the stone of witness mentioned in Joshua 24. 27. Both of these passages are also probably tinged with his hermetic notion of the sentience of rocks and stones—a conception that we find, without any Biblical reference, in *Man* (ll. 23–5). In addition he makes considerable use of the commonplace of God as the rock of ages, frequently fusing this with the image of the rock struck by Moses, as for instance in the lines,

> Yet Thou, the great eternal Rock
> Whose height above all ages shines,
> Art still the same, and canst unlock
> Thy waters to a soul that pines.
>
> *White Sunday*

It is, however, in the matter of language that Vaughan's chief indebtedness to the Bible lies. In its most general qualities his English is unquestionably that of the Authorized Version, tending always towards the simple and concrete in word and expression, sharing its vocabulary and to some extent its idioms. This influence of the Bible on his literary English must have been profound and enduring, for to say nothing of his intent and continuous reading of it in the days of his regeneration, we have his own word that in his earliest and most impressionable years

> Thou wert the first put in my hand,
> When yet I could not understand,
> And daily didst my young eyes lead
> To letters, till I learnt to read.
>
> *To The Holy Bible*

To speak more particularly, his poems are replete with phrases taken straight from the Bible. Consider, for instance, this passage in *Abel's Blood*, a poem that is a meditation on Genesis 4. 10 :

> A sea, whose loud waves cannot sleep,
> But *deep* still calleth upon *deep* :
> Whose urgent *sound*, like unto that
> *Of many waters*, beateth at
> The everlasting doors above,
> Where souls behind the altar move,
> And with one strong incessant cry
> Inquire '*How long?*' of the Most High.
> Almighty Judge! . . .[1]

Here 'deep [still] calleth [upon] deep' comes from Psalms 42. 7, 'sound of many waters' from Revelation 1. 15, 'everlasting doors' from Psalms 24. 7, and 'Most High' from numerous texts. Further, the last four lines of the extract, admittedly more of a loose quotation than an example of echoed phrases, originate in Revelation 6. 9–10 : '. . . I saw under the altar the souls of them that were slain for the word of God. . . . And they cried with a loud voice, saying, How long, O Lord, holy and true, dost thou not judge and avenge our blood on them that dwell on the earth.' So, too, in the third short stanza of *Righteousness*, the poem that immediately follows *Abel's Blood*, 'upright heart', 'single eye', 'clean, pure hands' and 'Invisibles' all echo—with some slight distortions—Biblical phrases.[2]

Though these two passages represent extreme examples of their kind, there are comparatively few poems in *Silex Scintillans* that are without at least one Scriptural phrase; and a full list of these borrowed phrases would be a very extensive one. Many of them (like most perhaps of the examples already given) will be immediately recognised; but even the reader who knows his Bible fairly well—unless he is doing some laborious elbow-work with a Concordance—may fail to realise that 'howling

[1] Vaughan's italics.

[2] For 'upright in heart' see numerous texts like Psal. 7. 10; 'if thine eye be single'—Matt. 6. 22; 'clean hands and a pure heart'—Psal. 24. 4; 'for the invisible things', etc.—1 Rom. 1. 20. In addition 'hidden treasures' in the same stanza is a recollection of Matt. 13. 44, and 'which never meddled pitch' echoes Eccles. 13. 1—'he that toucheth pitch shall be defiled'.

wilderness', a most suggestive phrase in *Providence*, is straight
from Deut. 32. 10, that 'the ground was curst' in the first
Dedication poem is probably an adaptation of 'cursed is the
ground' in Gen. 3. 17, and 'flaming ministry' in *The Search* certainly a distillation from Psalms 104. 4. But it is not only
Vaughan's impressive familiarity with all parts of the Bible that
produces these unrecognised verbal echoes. We are inclined to
accept them as original because they blend indistinguishably
with the rest of his highly Biblical English.

No doubt many of these Scriptural phrases were reproduced
quite unconsciously, without any intention of oblique or enriching effects. On the other hand, many of them were just as certainly employed for purposes of deliberate overtone, like 'City
of Palm trees' in *The Retreat*, which, pointing exactly to Deut.
34. 3, associates Vaughan's spiritual wanderings from the true
path with those of the Jews and Moses.[1] Further, Vaughan
sometimes uses a Biblical phrase (or quotation) to underline
some general allusion. Thus his reference to the Pentecostal fire
at the beginning of *White Sunday* includes 'cloven tongues'
(Acts 2. 3),[2] while his allusion to the Flood in *The Rainbow* contains the 'Heaven's windows' of *Gen.* 7. 11 and 8. 2. In much the
same way his intimation in *The British Church* of the perfect
marriage between Christ and his Church, the accepted allegorical reading of *The Song of Songs*, is brought out by a
modified phrase from that book, 'hills of myrrh and incense' (4.
6), and also by his later quotation:

> And haste Thee so
> As a young roe
> Upon the mounts of spices.[3]

Besides these phrase fragments there are numerous Biblical
quotations or near-quotations in the poems. Several of these,
like 'Would it were Day!' (Deut. 28. 67) in *Resurrection and*

---

[1] For further examples see the later studies of four main poems.

[2] The verb 'rush'd' that Vaughan uses with 'flames' in stanza 2 is probably an
unconscious echo of the 'rushing mighty wind' in the previous verse of Acts 2.

[3] See *The Song of Songs* 8. 14: 'Make haste, my beloved, and be thou like to a
roe or to a young hart upon the mountains of spices.'

Immortality (l. 68) and 'Thrust in thy sickle' (Rev. 14. 15) at the end of *Corruption*, Vaughan prints in italics, and four[1] bear footnote identification as well; but most of them have no distinguishing mark of any kind. Since he sometimes draws on out-of-the-way parts of the Bible and often modifies the wording of his original, it is easy to miss some of these quotations, which, like the phrases, are perfectly married to his own style. Only the reader working with a Concordance is likely to realise that 'Rise to prevent the Sun' at the beginning of *Rules and Lessons* (l. 11) is taken from the Apocryphal book of Wisdom (16.28) —'we must prevent the sun to give thee thanks'—or even that the line, 'The fields are long since white,' in *The Day of Judgment* (l. 13) comes from John 4. 35—'... look on the fields; for they are white already to harvest.'

The quotations are of all shapes and sizes. In length they range from the six-line extract in *The Men of War* from Revelation (obviously, along with *The Song of Songs* and the Epistle to the Romans, one of his favourite books) to lines and half lines like those just mentioned. Occasionally, as for example in the quotation from *The Song of Songs* that Vaughan incorporates in *Dressing* (ll. 2–3) and in *The Night* (ll. 32–3), he manages to keep fairly close to the words of his original. But since he is running prose into verse there is usually some word change in his quotations, and sometimes his alterations are quite considerable. For example his quotation in *Church Service* of Romans 8. 26 —'but the Spirit itself maketh intercession for us with groanings which cannot be uttered'—appears as

> The God above!
> And Holy Dove!
> With interceding, spiritual groans
> Make restless moans
> For dust, and stones....[2]

Here the quotation is a little longer than the original. At other times Vaughan compresses his borrowing, as for instance in the

---

[1] *The Stone, The Men of War, The Hidden Treasure* and *The Agreement*.
[2] See also the quotation in *Midnight*, ll. 29–32 of Psal. 147. 18.

line 'Green trees of life, and living streams' (*The Queer*, l. 8),
which is an intense distillation of Rev. 22. 1–2. Sometimes,
again, his quotations are almost paraphrases, as when the idea of
Job 25. 5—'yea, the stars are not pure in his sight' is reproduced
in *Repentance* as

> The heavens themselves, though fair and bright,
> Are dark and unclean in Thy sight.

Occasionally Vaughan transposes his quotation into a slightly
different context. Thus the *Isaiah* prophecy of the coming of the
blessed time when 'the mountains and the hills shall break forth
before you into singing' (55. 12) is adapted—with modified
phrasing—to form part of one of his familiar pictures of the
Creation in its morning 'Praise and Prayer':

> So hills and valleys into singing break;
> And though poor stones have neither speech nor tongue,
> While active winds and streams both run and speak,
> Yet stones are deep in admiration.

The Bird

But, in striking contrast with what happens to so many of his
quotations from Herbert, such changes[1] are rare and comparatively slight.

So far as the process of poetic writing and 'inspiration' is concerned, especially at the subconscious level, Vaughan's Biblical
echoes are far less interesting than those from Herbert. He
regarded the text of the Scriptures as sacred; it was readily
accessible to him (with a good deal probably known by heart);
and he had certainly spent much time, outside periods of poetic
composition, consciously pondering the references and quotations that he makes in his poems. Hence he usually manipulates
his borrowings in a simple, straightforward, and deliberate
manner.

However, there are a few exceptions to this general rule. One
is the last stanza of *The Shower*:

[1] Three other examples of a change of context are *The Retreat*, ll. 27–8, if this
echoes Job 12. 25 or Psal. 107. 27; *White Sunday*, l. 16, which refers to Job 29. 3;
and the passage quoted in the text from *Church Service*.

> Yet, if as thou dost melt, and with thy train
> Of drops make soft the Earth, my eyes could weep
> O'er my hard heart, that's bound up and asleep;
> Perhaps at last,
> Some such showers past,
> My God would give a sunshine after rain.

This passage is exceptional for the close integration of two separate quotations—Psalms 65. 10, 'Thou makest it [the Earth] soft with showers,' and 2 Samuel 23. 4, 'as the tender grass springing out of the earth by clear shining after rain.' Either of these quotations, and especially the second, could have been a subconscious recollection. But what is particularly interesting about their fusion here is the possibility that one brought the other by a process of association, since apart from the obvious rain-showers and soft-tender links, verse 10 of the Psalm also contains the word 'spring'—'thou blessest the springing thereof.'

Another interesting passage is to be found in two consecutive stanzas from *Ascension Hymn* :

> But since he
> That brightness soil'd,
> His garments be
> All dark and spoil'd,
> And here are left as nothing worth,
> Till the Refiner's fire breaks forth.

> Then comes He!
> Whose mighty light
> Made his clothes be
> Like heav'n, all bright;
> The Fuller, Whose pure blood did flow,
> To make stain'd man more white than snow.

In the first of these stanzas, where Vaughan is talking about fallen Man—and chiefly about his physical body—the Scriptural references are fairly straightforward : the third and fourth lines might be an echo of Jude, verse 23—'hating even the garment spotted by the flesh' (or just possibly of Isa. 64. 6); and the last line, quoting an exact phrase, 'Refiner's fire', is certainly a deliberate allusion to the well-known prophecy in Malachi (3. 2) concerning the coming of the Lord. ('Nothing worth' may be merely a casual recollection of a phrase in Job 24. 25; on the other hand, it may be a pointed reference to the Collect for Quinquagesima Sunday.)

The important quotation is the one from Malachi, for this has certainly generated much of the second stanza. 'Refiner's fire' is closely linked, in a compound simile, with 'fuller's soap', and though Vaughan has omitted this part of the verse in his quotation, it has recalled, by association, another well-known 'fuller' reference, the description of Christ's transfiguration, which he very loosely quotes in the second stanza—'And his raiment became shining, exceeding white as snow; so as no fuller on earth can white them' (Mark 9. 3). But the Fuller, crossed with the paradox of the whitening blood,[1] remains Christ, as in the original Malachi quotation, while the snow simile is shifted from the transfiguration of Christ to the state of redeemed man.

However, beyond any question, the most interesting of all Vaughan's Bible-inspired images is that of the Spirit, water, and blood, such as we find, for instance, in *Midnight*:

> Come then, my God!
> Shine on this blood
> And water, in one beam.

To understand this complex we must turn to *Trinity Sunday* and the New Testament text from which this poem is centrally derived:

> O holy, blessed, glorious Three,
> Eternal witnesses that be
> In heaven, one God in Trinity!
>
> As here on Earth, when men withstood,
> The Spirit, Water, and the Blood
> Made my Lord's Incarnation good:
>
> So let the antitypes in me
> Elected, bought, and seal'd for free,
> Be own'd, sav'd, sainted by you Three!

This is he that came by water and blood, even Jesus Christ; not by water only, but by water and blood. And it is the Spirit that beareth witness, because the Spirit is truth.

[1] See Rev. 7. 14. This paradox is repeated in the poem 'As Time one day', l. 36.

For there are three that bear record in heaven, the Father, the Word, and the Holy Ghost; and these three are one.

And there are three that bear witness in earth, the spirit, and the water, and the blood; and these three agree in one.   1 John 5. 6–8

With this New Testament reference and clues from other writings of Vaughan and his brother Thomas (who also attached great importance to this 1 John text[1]) we can interpret *Trinity Sunday* something as follows. The 'Spirit' is the divine in Christ, and probably also truth and revelation. Its antitype is man's soul, the divine spark. 'Blood', as well as signifying the man in Christ and man's physical nature, almost certainly alludes to the Passion and to Christ's sacrifice. More particularly still, Vaughan may have had in mind the verse in John 19, pointed to in the margin of the Authorized Version: 'But one of the soldiers with a spear pierced his side, and forthwith came there out blood and water' (v. 34).

'Water' signifies Christ's washing away of mortal sin, his sorrow for man and his 'saving tears' (always so vivid in Vaughan's imagination), the link with the fountains of life, and possibly what Thomas Vaughan describes as the *vehiculum* between heaven and earth.[2] The antitype of the Water in Christ is man's tears of repentance and—just conceivably—his passions and humours.

(We might diagrammatically represent Vaughan's water symbolism something as follows :[3]

	Fountains of life.	Heaven. Immortality.
↓ ↑	Exhalations. Rain. Showers. Dew. Christ's 'saving tears'.	Divine Grace, Love and Pity. Baptism. Prayer.
↓ ↑	Springs, streams, etc. (Puddles). Man's tears.	Repentance. Purification. Regeneration.)

[1] See *Anthroposophia Theomagica* (Waite's ed.), p. 4, and *Magia Adamica*, p. 142.
[2] The relevant passage from *Euphrates* is quoted on p. 74.
[3] This is of course the roughest kind of 'visual aid'. For simplicity the items have been selected, and some of them might be diagrammatically transposed.

From the above interpretation of *Trinity Sunday* it can be seen that this Spirit–water–blood complex, derived from a New Testament text that Vaughan, like his brother, had pondered deeply, is exceptionally rich in its religious implications. Further, the terms constitute a literal trinity, intimately and intricately linked, with 'water' and 'blood' to some extent interchangeable.

It is a measure of the vitality of this complex in Vaughan's poetic imagination that it constitutes, though less consciously treated perhaps than in *Trinity Sunday*, the plasm of two other poems. One of these is the short lyric, *Love-sick*,[1] which, opening with an invocation to Jesus, Spirit, grace—

> Jesus, my life! how shall I truly love Thee?
> O that Thy spirit would so strongly move me :
> That Thou wert pleas'd to shed Thy grace so far
> As to make man all pure love, flesh a star

—goes on to express a yearning for the tears of repentance—

> And at Thy presence make these mountains flow,
> These mountains of cold ice in me

—and concludes in the assurance of 'Thy blood which makes Thee mine'. Another interesting feature of the complex in this poem is that, like the lines already quoted from *Midnight*, it incorporates the notion of the Spirit as 'Refining fire'.

Closely akin to *Love-sick* is *The Storm*. Beginning with the lines,

> I see the Usk; and know my blood
> Is not a sea;[2]

the first two stanzas compare the poet's blood, or passions, with a turbulent, flooding river. Stanza two ends with the line,

> Breeds tempests in my blood;

and the third stanza, completing the full spirit–water–blood complex, presents an elaborate fusion of spirit, wind and blasts with

---

[1] *Love-sick*, which immediately precedes *Trinity Sunday* in the text of *Silex Scintillans*, may be closely connected with the latter poem in its date of composition.

[2] 'Usk' is Sir Edward Marsh's emendation for 'use'.

clouds and water, the whole symbolising regeneration and purification, Christ weeping and man upwards aspiring. The double
motion up and down, so to speak, is here most pronounced :

> Love, then round me with weeping clouds,
>   And let my mind
> In quick blasts sigh beneath those shrouds,
>   A spirit-wind;
> So shall that storm purge this recluse
>   Which sinful ease made foul,
> And wind and water to Thy use
>   Both wash and wing my soul.

Besides *Love-sick* and *The Storm*, there are more than a dozen
poems in which this same image complex is present in a more
subordinate fashion. Sometimes Vaughan elaborates it quite
deliberately, as for instance in the following lines from *The
Passion*, which are closely connected with the second stanza of
Trinity Sunday:

> O my chief good!
> My dear, dear *God*!
> When Thy best *blood*
> Did issue forth forc'd by the rod,
>   What pain didst Thou
>   Feel in each blow!
>   How didst Thou *weep*,
>   And Thyself steep
> In Thy own precious, saving *tears*!
>   What cruel smart
>   Did tear Thy heart!
>   How dist Thou groan it
>   In the *spirit*.[1]

On the other hand, though the complex is full of essential religious concepts, and derived from a much-meditated Scriptural
text, there appear to have been occasions when it emerged into
his poetry by some process of subconscious association. One of
these occasions was almost certainly the composition of *L'Envoy*,
where 'blood', 'spirits' and 'water' (the last a most unusual

---

[1] For other examples of a conscious use of the complex see the lines quoted in
the text from *Midnight*, *Misery*, ll. 105–11, and *Admission*, where the prayer for
Christ's heart (or spirit) to infuse the poet is followed by ll. 29–32.

similitude in Vaughan for sin) are all disparate terms, rather than parts of a unified whole :

> Incline each hard heart to do good,
> And cement us with Thy Son's *blood*;
> That like true sheep, all in one fold
> We may be fed, and one mind hold.
> Give watchful *spirits* to our guides :
> For sin—like *water*—hourly glides
> By each man's door. . . .

Similarly, in *Isaac's Marriage*, a subconscious association of words seems to have been at work as, after the description of Isaac's soul soaring upwards in prayer, Vaughan turns from the image of grace and response—

> and so returns the skies
> That *dew* they lent, a breathing sacrifice[1]

—to the opening of the next paragraph,

> Thus soar'd thy *soul*, who, though young, didst inherit
> Together with his *blood* thy father's *spirit*.

However, because the image complex contains a good deal of meditated substance it is often extremely difficult to decide whether its appearance in a poem is deliberately or subconsciously determined. Was Vaughan aware of its presence in *The Morning-Watch*, when, having completed the second syntactical movement with the line,

> This *dew* fell on my breast,

he continued with

> O how it *bloods*,
> And *spirits* all my earth!

And what are we to conclude about the composition of these lines in *Jesus Weeping I*?—

> Dear Jesus, weep on! pour this latter
> *Soul*-quick'ning *rain*, this living *water*
> On their dead hearts; but—O my fears!—
> They will drink *blood* that despise *tears*.

---

[1] 'Breathing', through the association of breath with spirit, may have played a subtle part in this linkage.

This problem is particularly teasing when one of the main terms is present only by implication. For instance, the blood–water antithesis at the close of *Easter-Day*—

> Arise! arise!
> And with His healing *blood* anoint thine eyes,
> Thy inward eyes; His *blood* will cure thy mind,
> Whose *spittle* only could restore the blind

—may be subconscious (or, some might say, purely fortuitous). But though the word 'spirit' is nowhere used, the whole poem is concerned with the resurrected Christ, while the Divine spirit as creative, warming fire and illumination is certainly evoked by the repeated sun image. Further, we must notice that the poem opens with a reference to tears—

> Thou, whose sad heart, and weeping head lies low.

There can be little doubt that the composition of *Easter-Day*, a poem that very closely follows an Herbert model, owes a good deal to the spirit–water–blood complex. But it is hard to say how conscious Vaughan was of what was happening in his imitation.[1]

Two further matters call for some brief comment in this discussion of the influence of Vaughan's Bible-reading on *Silex Scintillans*, the first being his metrical renderings of Psalms 65, 104, and 121.

On the whole these three pieces are quite undistinguished, and some of the writing in them is very limp indeed, especially when Vaughan is expanding his original to fill out his metrical pattern. One line certainly qualifies for inclusion among his worst—

> Chambers of rain, where heaven's large bottles lie.
>
> Psalm 104

On the other hand, there are one or two occasional felicities, like 'the comely spacious whale', which has a certain grotesque

[1] Four other passages comparable in this respect with *Easter-Day* are *St Mary Magdalen*, ll. 39–42, *The Rainbow*, ll. 26–30, *The Feast*, ll. 22–33, and *The Search*, ll. 34–40.

charm, and the sound and rhythmical suggestiveness of the two lines,

> Sailors that float on flowing seas
> Stand firm by Thee, and have sure peace.
>
> Psalm 65

There is nothing particularly revealing in Vaughan's choice of these three particular Psalms, though 65 and 104 must have been congenial for their large Nature references and their prominent water imagery. However, here and there, usually in the additions, his own religious attitude and individual sensibility are sometimes plainly evident. We notice, for example, how much more personal and intense than the Authorized Version translation ('Iniquities prevail against me : as for our transgressions, thou shalt purge them away') is his rendering of the third verse of Psalm 65 :

> But sinful words and works still spread
> And overrun my heart and head;
> Transgressions make me foul each day;
> O purge them, purge them all away!

The same Psalm contains the already quoted words, 'thou makest [the Earth] soft with showers; thou blessest the springings thereof' (v. 10), to which Vaughan characteristically adds the details of 'warm' rain, greenness, and 'unseen' growth :

> then Thy warm
> And opening showers—restrain'd from harm—
> Soften the mould, while all unseen
> The blade grows up alive and green.

So Vaughan-like is the last line and a half that it might very well have come from one of his own original poems; and the same lover of trees and vegetation is revealed in his version of Psalm 104, v. 16—'The trees of the Lord are full of sap; the cedars of Lebanon, which he hath planted'—where he changes 'sap' to 'greenness' and expands the second bare phrase with something that has been truly felt :

> Thou giv'st the trees their greenness, e'en to those
> Cedars in Lebanon, in whose thick boughs
> The birds their nests build.

There is a similar touch of native sensibility when, to the later phrase, 'it is night' (v. 20), he adds, 'In whose thick shades and silence . . . .' (l. 54).

Another interesting little change occurs with the opening of Psalm 121, which in the familiar words of the Authorized Version reads : 'I will lift up mine eyes unto the hills, from whence cometh my help. My help cometh from the Lord, which made heaven and earth'. Vaughan's version, though greatly inferior to this, is given his personal signature by the lyrical epithets that he adds to his favourite image of the hills of heaven, by his use of 'sigh', and by his substitution of an hermetic concept, the Divine spirit pervading Nature, for God the Creator :

> Up to those bright and gladsome hills,
>   Whence flows my weal and mirth,
> I look and sigh for Him Who fills,
>   Unseen, both heaven and earth.

The second matter concerns the versions of the Bible with which Vaughan was familiar.

No doubt that most of his quotations, in his prose works, as texts at the beginning and end of some of his poems, and included or closely echoed in his poetry, are drawn from the Authorized Version. On the other hand, there is clear evidence that he was acquainted with other translations. For example, the text (incorrectly given as Rom. 18. 19) that goes with *Man's Fall and Recovery* reads : 'As by the offence of one, the fault came on all men to condemnation; So by the Righteousness of one, the benefit abounded towards all men to the Justification of life.' This not only differs markedly from Rom. 5. 18 in the Authorized Version—'Therefore as by the offence of one judgment came upon all men to condemnation; even so by the righteousness of one the free gift came upon all men unto justification of life'—but is very close, even in punctuation, to the text in the Genevan Bible : 'Likewise then as by the offence of one, the fault came on all men to condemnation, so by the justifying of one, the benefit abounded toward all men to the justification of life.'

Another quotation that appears somewhat closer to the Genevan than to the Authorized Version is the text, *Hosea 6. 4*, that follows *Disorder and Frailty*:

VAUGHAN: 'O Ephraim what shall I do unto thee? O Judah how shall I intreat thee? for thy goodness is as a morning Cloud, and as the early Dew it goeth away.'

GENEVAN BIBLE: 'O Ephraim, what shall I do unto thee? O Judah, how shall I intreat thee? for your goodness is as a morning cloud, and as the morning dew it goeth away.'

AUTHORIZED VERSION: 'O Ephraim, what shall I do unto thee? O Judah, what shall I do unto thee? for your goodness is as a morning cloud, and as the early dew it goeth away.'

Finally, it is to be noticed that Vaughan was familiar with the Latin versions of Tremellius and Beza, the former providing him with his epigraph to *The British Church*, the latter with his text-heading to the poem 'And do they so?'

CHAPTER III

HERBERT'S POETRY

... that blessed man, Mr George Herbert, whose holy life and verses
gained many pious Converts (of whom I am the least) ....
Preface to Silex Scintillans.

SECOND only to the Bible among the outside forces that went to
the making of *Silex Scintillans* was George Herbert's poetry.
Indeed, so far as immediate stimulus is concerned, Herbert's
influence was even more decisive than that of the Bible, for without the inspiration and model of *The Temple* there would certainly have been no *Silex Scintillans*.

Apart from this incalculable initial impetus, Vaughan owed a
considerable debt to Herbert for the final establishment of his
style, after the false starts and variations of *Poems* and *Olor
Iscanus*; and in this consolidation perhaps nothing was more
important than Herbert's encouragement to the use of everyday
images. Occasionally we may observe him appropriating a particular image of this type. Thus Herbert's figure of the soul as a
room (with the linked metaphor of the key)—

> Only Thy Grace, which with these elements comes,
> Knoweth the ready way,
> And hath the privy key,
> Op'ning the soul's most subtle rooms
> The Holy Communion

—reappears in Vaughan's poem on the same subject as

> And with Thy secret key
> Open my desolate rooms.
> Dressing

But much more important than the particular images of this kind
that Vaughan borrowed from time to time was the continuous
general pressure from Herbert towards a homely type of imagery
and expression—an outstanding feature of his writing that

Vaughan, intent on composing in a similar strain of 'true, unfeigned, verse', may very well have regarded as one of the prime secrets of his beloved master. Certainly there is very little imagery of everyday life in the pre-*Silex Scintillans* poems, and still less that is used for the communication of serious ideas and emotions.

In themes, attitudes, and spirit, on the other hand, the poems of *Silex Scintillans* owe little to Herbert.[1] Admittedly there is some derivativeness—enough to give colour to the argument of certain critics who have exaggerated this side of Herbert's influence. For instance, Vaughan's persistent thought of the restless and unrooted life of mortal man and of the tiredness that is God's way of bringing him to salvation is also unmistakably Herbert's, and it produces a fundamental thematic similarity between *The Pursuit* and *Man* and Herbert's *Giddiness* and *The Pulley*. Again, there are two poems, *The Storm* and *Easter-Day* (and perhaps a third, *Son-Days*), so close to Herbert originals that they must be described as imitations : indeed *Easter-Day* is not so much a variation on a borrowed theme as a continuous variation, from beginning to end, on all the lines of Herbert's *The Dawning*.

Yet even in the few instances where Vaughan comes near to Herbert in the substance of his poem he usually produces an individual work that contains more of himself than of his master. Consider, for example, one of his two undoubted imitations, *The Storm*. On the one hand, this poem consists largely of a variation on the idea of the first three lines of Herbert's poem of the same name—

> If as the winds and waters here below
> > Do fly and flow,
> My sighs and tears as busy were above

—and also on the thought of the concluding couplet—

> Poets have wrong'd poor storms: such days are best;
> They purge the air without, within the breast.

[1] For critics who have taken a different view see W. Lewis Bettany, Introduction to his edition of *Silex Scintillans*, p. xxxiii; H. Grierson, Introduction, *Metaphysical Poetry, Donne to Butler*, p. xliv; and D. Bush, *English Literature in the Earlier Seventeenth Century*, p. 145.

In addition there is a good deal of verbal reminiscence. Thus the couplet just quoted is unmistakably echoed by Vaughan in his line,

> So shall that storm purge this recluse. . . .

On the other hand, while Vaughan's lyric has grown out of Herbert's, it also has a life and individuality of its own, so that it is no mere lifeless copy. For one thing, drawing on his personal observation of Nature, Vaughan typically makes much more of the literal 'storm' than Herbert does, and the whole of his first stanza is largely descriptive in effect. For another, less daring than his master, he drops Herbert's primary 'storm' idea —of assault, of forcing oneself on God—and throws more stress on the 'storm' of spiritual purgation, with a correspondingly more elaborate treatment of the winds and water, sighs and tears, conceit. Where Herbert's attitude is objective, his is personal; and while his stanza form owes something to his model, he has characteristically lengthened it to produce a different music.

'I walk'd the other day', because it is an incomparably finer work than *The Storm*, affords an even more striking instance of Vaughan's ability to breathe individual life into a poem that owes much more to Herbert than a few borrowed phrases.

There is no doubt that the lyric is a derivative poem. In its stanza form and treatment of subject, especially in the opening narrative pattern, it is unquestionably based on Herbert's *Peace* (from which Vaughan has also borrowed the phrase 'a gallant flower'). Further, the third stanza—

> Then taking up what I could nearest spy,
> I digg'd about
> That place where I had seen him to grow out;
> And by and by
> I saw the warm recluse alone to lie,
> Where fresh and green
> He liv'd of us unseen

—is clearly a recollection, even if a subconscious one, of what Herbert has written in *The Flower*:

> Who would have thought my shrivell'd heart
> Could have recover'd greenness ? It was gone
> Quite under ground; as flowers depart
> To see their mother-root, when they have blown;
> Where they together
> All the hard weather,
> Dead to the world, keep house unknown.

However, once more, even where the two poets converge most closely they remain individually distinctive. There is nothing in Vaughan's third stanza comparable with Herbert's purely emblematic treatment of his discovered, dug-up flower in the third stanza of *Peace* :

> Then went I to a garden, and did spy
> A gallant flower,
> The Crown Imperial : Sure, said I,
> Peace at the root must dwell.
> But when I digged, I saw a worm devour
> What show'd so well.

Again, granted the recollection of *The Flower* in Vaughan's third stanza, it is still the product of an individual sensibility—of one who had little or no regard for 'blown' flowers, who possessed a peculiar sense, which Herbert did not share, of the greenness and secret life of buried and apparently dead things, and whose habitual rhythm (as the above extracts indicate) was a looser, longer-breathed measure than Herbert's short, compact cadences. Further, in its chief communication, its note of personal bereavement, its moving affirmation of Vaughan's belief in immortality, which for once includes a passing mood of doubt, and its impressive and important statement of his attitude to the 'masques and shadows' of Nature, the poem is an entirely independent work, standing quite apart from either *Peace* or *The Flower*. These two poems may have stimulated Vaughan; they certainly did not beguile him into imitation.

Of the other suggested parallels of theme and subject-matter between the two poets—and these are not numerous anyway—none is particularly striking. *Rules and Lessons*, in its broad homiletic purpose (as well as its metrical form), was no doubt inspired by *The Church-Porch*, and some of Vaughan's teaching, on alms-giving and lewd speech, for instance, corresponds with what Herbert says in his poem. But where Herbert's much longer work is firmly and comprehensively based on the seven deadly sins, Vaughan completely ignores the themes of lust, drunkenness, lies, and sloth. Herbert's attention is fixed continuously on everyday life and concerns and on many secular activities that hardly come within the province of Christian morality. There is nothing of such matters in *Rules and Lessons*. On the other hand, *The Church-Porch* reveals nothing of the awareness of Nature that is evident in *Rules and Lessons*, and nothing, on this occasion, of the sensibility and imagination with which Vaughan informs his poem.

Much the same is to be said about the parallels of theme that W. Lewis Bettany suggested between *The Tempest* and *Misery* and between *The Ornament* and *The Quip*.[1] Admittedly *The Tempest* does owe an exceptionally heavy debt of word and image to *Misery*, while there is certainly some slight similarity of thought between the two poems, especially that of the spiritual perversity and blindness of man; but the stress that Vaughan throws on the lessons of Nature makes the difference between the two poems far more striking than the resemblance. Again, though *The Ornament* was probably inspired by *The Quip*, for both poems have a similar opening, and both express conflict between the austerity of the poet and the appetites of the 'merry world', Vaughan's poem has a much narrower range of reference than Herbert's, being simply an elaboration of the lines,

> Then came brave Glory puffing by
> In silks that whistled.

Finally, there is a very evident relationship between Vaughan's *The Match* and Herbert's *Obedience*. Vaughan's words,

> Here I join hands, and thrust my stubborn heart
> Into thy deed,

are unmistakably an answer to Herbert's aspiration:

[1] W. Lewis Bettany, *op. cit.*, p. 370 and pp. 386–7.

How happy were my part,
If some kind man would thrust his heart
Into these lines.

Each poem expresses the theme of absolute resignation to God's will, and Vaughan's contains three certain and substantial verbal echoes of Herbert. Yet when all these correspondences are fully revealed, both poems remain quite distinctive.

One further general point before we leave this question of the similarity of poetic themes between the two poets. If we are to see this resemblance (such as it is) in its right perspective we must always remember that both poets were, after all, writing in the same Christian tradition and communion. For example, it is inevitable, and in no way remarkable, that Vaughan's *The Passion* and Herbert's *The Agony* turn on the same ideas of the profound sinfulness of man and the suffering, infinite love of Christ.

So far we have been considering the general aspects of Herbert's influence on Vaughan, and these, though considerable, are difficult to assess with any certainty. In estimating Vaughan's more particular and tangible debts we can, however, be much more precise.

To begin with a very small example, there are twenty-six titles (these mainly in Part I of *Silex Scintillans*) that he has appropriated from *The Temple*,[1] as well as numerous others that have a strong Herbert flavour. But this debt deserves no more than passing mention, for only seven or eight pairs of the poems concerned have anything in common, and these similarities are never of any great consequence. The two poems on *Faith* and the two on *Affliction* perhaps bear some slight resemblance in idea and sentiment; *Praise* and *Trinity-Sunday* have the same metrical form[2] as their Herbert namesakes; and in *The Wreath*

---

[1] The twenty-six poems are: *Death, The Search, The British Church, The Call, Content, The Storm, Peace, Holy Scriptures, Son-days, Repentance, Faith, The Dawning, Praise, Holy Communion, Affliction, The Pilgrimage, The World, Misery, Man, White Sunday, The Star, Trinity Sunday, The Jews, Providence, St Mary Magdalen, The Wreath*.

[2] There is also some slight resemblance between the stanza forms of the two poems entitled *The Star*.

Vaughan has employed the rhetorical device of an intertwining, repeated phrase between the end of one line and the beginning of the next that Herbert uses in *A Wreath*.[1]

As well as *Praise* and *Trinity-Sunday*, *Rules and Lessons* and *Easter-Day* also owe their metrical forms to Herbert;[2] and there are several other pieces that were probably metrical adaptations of an Herbert original—*The Storm* from the poem of the same name, *White Sunday* from *Whitsunday*, *Righteousness* from *Constancy*,[3] 'I walk'd the other day' from *Peace* (and possibly *The Flower*) and *Begging I* from *Praise*. It is likely, too, that Herbert's example encouraged Vaughan's predilection in *Silex Scintillans* for the fairly elaborate stanza form of varied line-length and rhyme-pattern, though it is notable—and significant of the fundamental rhythmical difference between the two poets —that Vaughan commonly employs a longer stanza than Herbert, who very rarely writes in an eight- or ten-line measure. Also, apart from *The Collar*, there is no Herbert model for the continuous form of diversified line-length and rhyme that Vaughan uses in such poems as *Resurrection and Immortality*.

Another small trace of Herbert's influence is to be discerned in the opening of many of Vaughan's poems. Like Herbert (and of course Donne) Vaughan is fond of an arresting type of opening—some short exclamation or question or dramatic statement that jolts and surprises us into instant attention. Sometimes, as again with Herbert, openings of this sort create the illusion of an argument or discussion that has been caught up in mid-career. And, in addition to sharing this general metaphysical family resemblance, a number of Vaughan's first lines echo Herbert's own words. Three poems (*The Passion*, *The Resolve*, and *The Palm Tree*) start with an exact quotation of one of Herbert's opening lines,[4] and six others (*The Morning-Watch*,

---

[1] Vaughan uses the same rhetorical turn in *Love-sick*.

[2] *Rules and Lessons* is based on *The Church Porch*, and *Easter Day* on *The Dawning*, of which it is an exceptionally close imitation.

[3] In *Righteousness* Vaughan also follows to a large extent the rhetorical pattern of *Constancy*.

[4] *The Passion* from *Good-Friday*, *The Resolve* from *The Reprisal*, *The Palm Tree* from *Love Unknown*.

Unprofitableness, Praise, Easter-Day, The Holy Communion and
Begging I) with a slightly modified one,[1] while for the beginning of *Admission* and *The Tempest* ('How shrill are silent
tears!' and 'How is man parcell'd out!') Vaughan has
adapted a phrase from the body of *The Family* and *Love I*
respectively.

These borrowed openings constitute just one example of
Vaughan's main tangible indebtedness to Herbert, which is to be
traced in his expression and imagery. Another is the sizable
group of single words, frequently bearing some unusual form or
shade of meaning, whose presence in *Silex Scintillans* is chiefly
due to Herbert's usage—words like 'crumb' (or 'crumb'd'),
'interline', 'leiger', 'snudge', and the three approximate synonyms 'aim', 'mean', and 'threaten'.[2] Besides this there are some
thirty instances where Vaughan has casually appropriated,
usually without point or respect for the context, some Herbert
phrase or turn of expression, like 'silent tear', 'full-ey'd love',
'Work and wind', 'break thy fence', and 'challenge here the
brightest day'.[3]

However, these items are slight beside Vaughan's frequent
borrowings of whole lines and short passages, many of which
must have been supplied either by a good memory or recourse
to Herbert's pages, for they are extremely close to their

[1] For *The Morning-Watch* see *The Holy Scriptures I*, for *Unprofitableness The Flower*, for *Praise* and *Begging I Praise II*, for *Easter-Day The Dawning*, and for *The Holy Communion The Banquet*.

[2] 'Interline' (*White Sunday*) means 'get between the lines, appear'; 'leiger' (*Corruption*) a permanent ambassador or representative; 'snudge' (*Misery*) 'to live in a miserly way or walk in a stooping or meditative attitude'. The three synonyms have the general meaning of, to purpose, intend, aim at. The difficult one of the three is 'threaten' (Vaughan's *Disorder and Frailty* and Herbert's *The Hold-fast*). L. L. Martz (*op. cit.*, footnote, p. 134) confesses difficulty in glossing the cognate 'threatenings' in *The Cross*. I think he is wrong in suggesting 'offerings'. The more probable meaning is 'intentions', parallel with 'designs' in the previous line. Had 'threaten', like 'white', some Welsh turn of meaning with which both Herbert and Vaughan were familiar?

[3] 'Silent tear' ('Thou that knowst' and *Admission*) from Herbert's *The Family*; 'full-ey'd love' (*Cock-Crowing*) from *The Glance*; 'work and wind' (*Midnight* and *Misery*) from *Jordan II*; 'break thy fence' (*The Law and the Gospel*) from *The Church Porch*; 'challenge here the brightest day' (*The Relapse*) from *Confession*.

originals and unquestionably deliberate. Here are three examples out of a considerable number :[1]

[1]

An ancient way,
All strewed with flowers and happiness,
And fresh as May.

The Resolve

I had my wish and way :
My days were strew'd with flow'rs and happiness :
There was no month but May.[2]

Affliction I

[2]

Profaneness on my tongue doth rest,
Defects and darkness in my breast.

Repentance

Profaneness in my head,
Defects and darkness in my breast.

Aaron

[3]

Rain gently spreads his honey-drops, and pours
Balm on the cleft earth, milk on grass and flowers.

The Rainbow

Rain, do not hurt my flowers; but gently spend
Your honey drops.

Providence

In addition to these fairly exact quotations there are numerous short passages in *Silex Scintillans* that echo Herbert in more

---

[1] In the text the Vaughan quotations are followed by the Herbert originals. Other examples of this kind of quotation are: *The Passion*, ll. 15–20, and *The Agony*, l. 11 and ll. 13–14 and ll. 17–18; *The Match*, Part II, ll. 7–10, and *Love Unknown*, ll. 3–5; *Holy Scriptures*, ll. 3–4, and *Whitsunday*, ll. 1–4; *Affliction*, ll. 35–40, and *The Temper I*, ll. 22–4; *Retirement*, ll. 45–8, and *Church Monuments*, ll. 6–9 and ll. 17–18; *The Sap*, ll. 17–18 and ll. 21–2, and *Business*, ll. 20–2 and ll. 26–28; *Begging II*, ll. 13–16, and *Nature*, ll. 4–6; *Palm Sunday*, ll. 35–8, and *Easter*, ll. 19–22.

[2] Vaughan also quotes this line, more closely, in *Providence*, l. 18.

indirect, though usually unmistakable, ways. In these passages, better described as reminiscences and allusions than as quotations, Vaughan makes more contribution of his own, while the phrasing of the original is often considerably modified and occasionally ignored altogether. The difference between the two types of reference may be conveniently illustrated by two of his borrowings from *Church Monuments*. In his *Retirement* he writes :

> A faithful school, where thou may'st see,
>> In heraldry
>> Of stones and speechless earth,
>> Thy true descent. . . .

These lines may be described as a quotation from *Church Monuments*, though the quotation is looser than usual and fuses two separate passages from Herbert's poem :

> Therefore I gladly trust
> My body to this school, that it may learn
> To spell his elements, and find his birth
> Written in dusty heraldry and lines. . . .

> Dear flesh, while I do pray, learn here thy stem
> And true descent. . . .

On the other hand, when Vaughan recalls this same Herbert poem in his *Burial*, his echo is of a remote and oblique kind—a repetition of single, disparate words in a generally similar context of the whirlwind of death :

> [1]
> Thou art the same, faithful and just
>> In life, or *dust*.
> Though then, thus crumm'd, I stray
>> In *blasts*,
>> Or *exhalations*, and wastes,
>> Beyond all eyes,
>> Yet Thy love spies
> That change, and knows Thy clay.

Burial

[2]

Here I entomb my flesh, that it betimes
May take acquaintance of this heap of *dust*;
To which the *blast* of death's incessant motion,
Fed with the *exhalation* of our crimes,
Drives all at last.

Church Monuments

No doubt in many of the parallels of this second kind Vaughan was still consciously recollecting Herbert's poems: we have reminiscences rather than quotations because his memory of the original was defective. But a close examination of all the parallel passages strongly suggests that many of the reminiscences are of a subconscious type. For instance, in the passage just quoted from *Burial* the detailed contexts of Vaughan's 'dust', 'blasts', and 'exhalations' are quite different from Herbert's, and one can only think that Vaughan's dominant idea of the whirlwind of death had, by some curious subconscious process, called up a cluster of words that Herbert had used to express a similar thought. Again, only some such process of association will account for the fact that a phrase from Herbert's *The Star*—'thy celestial quickness'—reappears in one of Vaughan's poems about stars in the disjunctive form of

O what bright *quickness*,
Active brightness,
And *celestial* flows. . . .

Midnight

As a further example of a probably subconscious echo one might instance—largely because of Vaughan's severance of 'wing' and 'groan'—the parallel between the elegy 'Thou that know'st' and *Sion* :

A silent tear can pierce Thy throne,
When loud joys want a wing;
And sweeter airs stream from a groan,
Than any arted string.

'Thou that know'st'

61

But groans are quick, and full of wings,
And all their motions upward be;
And ever as they mount, like larks they sing;
The note is sad, yet music for a King.

Sion

The fact that Vaughan's lines, through the quotation 'silent tear' are also linked with the fifth stanza of *The Family* clearly shows that we have something more than a simple, straightforward, and conscious allusion, and it appears probable that the familiar Herbert idea of the music of grief, which Vaughan would certainly have known in a conscious way, brought with it on this occasion a rich but shadowy margin of mainly subconscious associations.

This last example, if a somewhat obscure one, brings us to a particularly interesting feature about Vaughan's borrowings from Herbert—the way in which some deliberate reference (often a quotation) will frequently carry with it an active associational fringe of a subconscious kind. Consider, for example, *Disorder and Frailty*. The third stanza of this poem contains an 'exhalation' image that was almost certainly a fairly conscious borrowing from Herbert's poem *The Answer* (ll. 8–12) since Vaughan employs it on several occasions. Now just before the parallel Herbert lines, with no necessary relation to them or to each other, occur the two minor images of 'leaves' and 'flies'—

all the thoughts and ends,
Which my fierce youth did bandy, fall and flow
Like leaves about me; or like summer friends,
Flies of estates and sunshine.

It seems most likely that Vaughan's recollection of the 'exhalation' image somehow drew along with it, as vague subconscious material to be combined and worked up anew, just these two images of the 'leaves' and the 'flies', since his poem also has (in a passage that cannot be quotation or reference) the lines,

Each fly doth taste,
Poison and blast
My yielding leaves.

His poem *Misery* affords another clear example of this process. Line 96—'To look him out of all his pain'—is a fairly close and straightforward quotation from a line in the last stanza of Herbert's *The Glance*. But this Herbert stanza must have given Vaughan, subconsciously, much more than his deliberate quotation, for the word-stuff of its opening—

> If Thy first *glance* so powerful be,
> A mirth but *open'd* and *seal'd* up again

—reappears, quite randomly, in

> And with one *glance*,—could he that gain—
> To look him out of all his pain. . . .
> *Open* my rocky heart, and fill
> It with obedience to Thy will;
> Then *seal* it up. . . .

Since another phrase from Herbert's last stanza, 'full-ey'd love', turns up in *Cock-Crowing*, it may well be that Vaughan had the stanza to some extent by heart; but even if this were the case, his repetition of the words 'glance', 'open'd', and 'seal'd' must have occurred without his realisation of what was happening. Involuntarily, he was under the control of Herbert's lines.

Again, though it is difficult to decide which was the conscious recollection and which the associational fringe, there seems little doubt that one or other of the sequent but unconnected items near the beginning of Herbert's poem *The Glimpse*—

> Methinks delight should have
> More skill in music, and keep better time.
> Wert thou a wind or wave. . . .

exercised a subconscious effect on the first paragraph of Vaughan's *Joy*, which begins with a reference to music (the main theme of the paragraph)—

> Be dumb, coarse measures, jar no more; to me
> There is no discord but your harmony, etc.

—and a little later has the line

A lesson play'd him by a wind or wave.[1]

There remain several other features of Vaughan's Herbert echoes to be briefly noted. One is the way two recollections are occasionally fused together in the same passage. A complex and interesting example of this kind occurs in the second stanza of *Christ's Nativity*:

> Awake, awake! hark how th' wood rings,
> Winds whisper, and the busy springs
> A consort make;
> Awake! awake!
> Man is their high-priest, and should rise
> To offer up the sacrifice.

These lines are a combination (possibly with some of the sub-conscious associations we have just been considering) of

> Hark, how the birds do sing,
> And woods do ring,
>
> *Man's Medley*

and of

> Man is the world's High Priest: he doth present
> The sacrifice for all; while they below
> Unto the service mutter an assent,
> Such as springs use that fall, and winds that blow.
>
> *Providence*

The incidence of the parallels varies considerably; and here the most significant point to appreciate is that they are four times as numerous in Part I as in Part II.[2] The reason for this

---

[1] Other probable instances of this phenomenon occur in the opening of *Religion* where the echo in stanza 2 of Herbert's *Decay*, ll. 6–7, appears to carry the references to Jacob and Abraham; in *The Incarnation and Passion* where the echo in ll. 1–2 of *The Bag*, ll. 10–12, brings with it the 'story' reference; and in *Admission* where the connection in stanza 1 between 'silent tears' and 'Marble sweats, And rocks have tears' is suggested by Herbert's allusions to weeping marble (*The Church Floor* and 'Grieve not the Holy Spirit'). In at least one other instance the associational fringe may have been one of sound suggestion. Compare 'Life's but a *blast*, he knows it' (*The Tempest*, l. 49) with 'Man is but *grass*, He knows it' (*Misery*, ll. 5–6).

[2] Both L. C. Martin (Commentary, *Vaughan's Works*, second ed.) and W. Lewis Bettany in his edition of *Silex Scintillans* agree with this proportion.

difference is not hard to find. The year or two in which Vaughan composed the poems of Part I was a period in which Herbert's poetry made a tremendous impact on his imagination—when he probably read and pondered *The Temple* with the same reverential attention that he gave to his meditation on the Scriptures, when he may have been in the habit of reading a few of its pages before composing (as Gray read Spenser), when he had a good deal of Herbert's work by heart (or nearly so), and when it was almost impossible for him to write a poem without some echo, in word or image, of the master. Between 1650 and 1654 this pressure, though still strong, was inevitably diminishing: he probably read Herbert less regularly and with less of that stimulating excitement of first, decisive encounter, while verbal memory of what Herbert had written was probably growing fainter. We should, after all, hardly expect a single inspirational impulse of this kind to last undiminished for six or seven years, especially in a poet who had much of his own to say.

Of the sixty-odd poems, in both parts of *Silex Scintillans*, that contain some Herbert echo rather more than half carry a single parallel, often a mere phrase. In the remaining poems of this group the incidence of quotation and reminiscence varies greatly, and there are three poems, *Son-Days*, *The Tempest* and *Retirement* (all significantly in Part I), that are quite exceptional in the number of their Herbert recollections. In *Retirement*, which, as one critic rightly says,[1] might be taken for one of Herbert's minor poems, there are at least five parallels, and in *The Tempest* eight,[2] three of these with *Misery*.

The range of parallels is about the same on each side, for the

---

[1] J. M. Summers, *George Herbert: His Religion and Art*, p. 199. The parallels are: 'throne of azure' (l. 1) with *Humility* (l. 2); l. 18, 'And would not see, but chose to wink', with *The Collar* (l. 26); l. 22, 'My love-twist' etc., with *The Pearl* (l. 16); ll. 45–8, 'A faithful school etc.', with *Church Monuments* (ll. 6–9 and ll. 17–18; and l. 55 with *The Collar* (l. 36). Also, as Summers observes, *Retirement* is exceptionally close to Herbert in its general tone and logical structure.

[2] L. 1 with *Love I*, l. 3; ll. 10–16 with *The Answer*, ll. 8–12; ll. 31–2 with *The Star*, ll. 17–18; l. 45 with *Misery*, l. 46; ll. 45–6 with *Man's Medley*, ll. 16–18; l. 49 with *Misery*, ll. 5–6; l. 49 with *The Collar*, l. 14, etc.; l. 53 with *Misery*, l. 49. Possibly, too, as Bettany suggests (p. 370) we may trace something of a parallel between ll. 37–40 and *Misery*, ll. 59–62.

sixty-odd reminiscences cover about fifty of Herbert's poems. At the same time it seems that Vaughan knew some of Herbert's pieces, like *Affliction I, Giddiness, Misery, Peace, Providence, The Church-Porch, The Flower, The Star,* and *Whitsunday,* with a special intimacy. For example, out of the eight stanzas of *The Star,* no less than five are unmistakably echoed in various Vaughan poems. It is also notable that a small number of Herbert passages, including the 'hatched' soul and 'exhalation' images, the flowers and carvings of Solomon's temple, the light-motion-heat trinity, and medicinal flowers, are echoed several times.[1]

Very occasionally Vaughan compresses his borrowing. Thus Herbert's lines in *Whitsunday,*

> Listen, sweet Dove, unto my song,
> And spread thy golden wings in me;
> Hatching my tender heart so long,
> Till it get wing, and fly away with thee,

emerge in *Holy Scriptures* as

> the Dove's spotless nest,
> Where souls are hatch'd unto eternity.

But in general Vaughan tends to expansion and diffusion, as when Herbert's idea in *The Temper I*—

> Stretch or contract me, Thy poor debtor:
> This is but tuning of my breast,
> To make the music better

—becomes in *Affliction,*

> Thus doth God key disorder'd man,
> Which none else can,
> Tuning his breast to rise or fall;
> And by a sacred, needful art
> Like strings stretch ev'ry part,
> Making the whole most musical.

[1] Herbert, *Whitsunday,* ll. 1–4, and Vaughan, *Holy Scriptures,* ll. 3–4, and *Disorder and Frailty,* ll. 46–9; Herbert, *The Answer,* ll. 8–12, and Vaughan, *Isaac's Marriage,* ll. 53–7, *The Shower,* ll. 1–6, *Disorder and Frailty,* ll. 31–7, *The Tempest,* ll. 10–16; Herbert, *Sion,* ll. 1–5, and Vaughan, *The Palm Tree,* ll. 9–12 and *The Night,* ll. 19–20; Herbert, *The Star,* ll. 17–18, and Vaughan, *The Lamp,* ll. 9–13, *Faith,* ll. 33–4, *The Tempest,* ll. 31–2, *Love-sick,* ll. 12–15; Herbert, *Life,* ll. 13–15, and Vaughan, *Childhood,* ll. 14–16, and *Death II,* ll. 21–5.

However, this feature of the borrowings must not be indiscriminately pressed as evidence for the commonplace (and in the main valid) distinction between the artistic compactness of Herbert and the undisciplined diffuseness of Vaughan. As we have seen, Vaughan is often recollecting Herbert remotely or subconsciously, and in this kind of recollection it is inevitable that Herbert's words, phrases, and images are sometimes slightly dispersed.

Approximately half of the poems in *Silex Scintillans* bear some discernible traces of Herbert's influence, and it is not surprising therefore if comprehensive lists of parallels between the two poets, like W. Lewis Bettany's or L. C. Martin's, create the impression that it is impossible to read Vaughan's work without hearing all the time the sweet, ghostly whisper of Herbert—worse, that a considerable amount of imitation went into the writing of *Silex Scintillans*.

Nevertheless, for two good reasons, this is an entirely mistaken impression. In the first place—to say nothing of the fact that the Herbert echoes are far less obtrusive in Part II than they are in Part I—it so happens that the finest of Vaughan's poems, those that we know him most intimately by and that chiefly constitute his richly individual 'world', are on the whole the ones in which Herbert's presence is least felt. The following is a list of poems, likely to be in any select anthology of most of us, that contain nothing, or only the slightest trace, of Herbert: *Regeneration*, *The Retreat*, 'Joy of my life', *Peace*, 'And do they so?', *Unprofitableness*, *The Burial of an Infant*, *The Dawning*, *Ascension-Day* and *Ascension-Hymn*, 'They are all gone into the world of light', *Cock-Crowing*, *The Timber*, *The Seed Growing Secretly*, 'As Time one day', *The Dwelling-Place*, *Childhood*, *The Night*, *The Waterfall*, *Quickness*. Admittedly, some notable exclusions have to be made from this list like *The Morning-Watch*, *The World*, *Man*, 'I walk'd the other day' (all in Part I), and *The Star*; all the same the list is a large and striking one.

In the second place, more often than not Vaughan adapts and

transforms his borrowings to a different context, frequently in radical and surprising ways. As Miss Elizabeth Holmes has well said: 'the reader who goes further perceives before long the deeper difference [between Herbert and Vaughan]; he finds him at rare moments transforming his borrowings, giving them a new dress that quite alters their aspect; or finds him in those remoter places where Herbert never came.'[1]

An excellent example of Vaughan's transformation of his borrowings occurs in one of the earliest poems of *Silex Scintillans*, *The Lamp*. The admirable opening lines of this lyric—

> 'Tis dead night round about: Horror doth creep
> And move on with the shades; stars nod and sleep

—carry in the phrase 'stars nod and sleep' a direct quotation from Herbert's *Divinity*. Now this phrase certainly bears some slight emotive quality, of fearful association, in Herbert's opening line—

> As men, for fear the stars should sleep and nod;

but in the main its connotation, and context, is a cool, intellectual one in which Herbert is establishing a parallel between the abstractions of astronomy and divinity. Vaughan, on the other hand, has incorporated the phrase in a descriptive passage that is full of intense emotional and sensuous effect, and thereby invested it with a force and richness that it lacks in Herbert's poem. We dwell on it in *The Lamp* where we barely notice it in *Divinity*. Even Vaughan's slight modification of the word-order, his placing of the weightier 'sleep' after 'nod', has effected a significant change.

In *The Resolve* we have another adaptation of Herbert, which, though it does not improve on the original as the borrowing in *The Lamp* does, is perhaps more radical. The lines already quoted (p. 59) are a symbolical description of the established way of righteousness, and they are closely akin to the opening of Vaughan's later poem of that name. But in the Herbert original the May-time and the flower-strewn way stand for

---

[1] *Henry Vaughan and the Hermetic Philosophy*, p. 14.

something very different: they represent the initial and transient phase of Herbert's religious experience before he had suffered the necessary discipline of the time when 'Sorrow was all my soul'.

Several of the other parallels that have already been quoted contain similar examples of marked transformation. For instance, the dove-hatched soul image (p. 66), one of the sequence of conceits that makes up the first part of *Holy Scriptures*, is in Herbert the invocation to a poem on the subject of Whitsunday. Again, where in *Joy* (p. 63-4) Vaughan echoes the phrase 'wind or wave' from Herbert's *The Glimpse*, he is setting it in contrast with the 'false, juggling sounds' of song and music: it signifies something that is part of the 'lesson' of Nature. But though there is a reference to music in the Herbert context, Herbert's 'wind or wave' is brought in to illustrate the fluctuations of delight.

Besides making these important changes and contributions of his own, Vaughan usually assimilates his borrowings with complete success into the rhythms and metrical forms, the characteristic diction, imagery, and ideas of his own compositions. It is very rare indeed that any Herbert fragment, whether we recognise it as such or not, grits with discordance. By and large, Vaughan only took from Herbert what was already in his own thought and sensibility. As Dowden once wrote: 'The thoughts and phrases of Herbert which he transfers to his own verse seem less an appropriation than an inheritance.'[1]

Sometimes in his borrowings Vaughan certainly improved on his original. Apart from *The Lamp* example, his lines in *Son-Days*,

> lamps that light
> Man through his heap of dark days,

read much better, for their simple vividness of phrasing and rhythmical subtlety, than their probable original in Herbert's *Sunday*:

[1] *Puritan and Anglican*, p. 120.

> The week were dark, but for thy light :
> Thy torch doth show the way.

But these undoubted improvements are not numerous and have to be weighed against other instances in which Vaughan's version is definitely inferior to Herbert's, as in the parallel between *Affliction* and *The Temper I* (p. 66) or in that between Herbert's *Whitsunday* (quoted p. 66) and Vaughan's other version of this image, slack in rhythm and phrasing, in *Disorder and Frailty* :

> O, yes! but give wings to my fire,
> And hatch my soul, until it fly
> Up where Thou art, amongst Thy tire
> Of stars, above infirmity.

However, though a few writers have stressed these weaker imitations,[1] usually there is very little to choose between the corresponding passages.

All considered, there can be little doubt that Herbert's poetry exercised an immense influence on the composition of *Silex Scintillans*. On the other hand, in spite of this great indebtedness to *The Temple*, Vaughan's work, particularly the flower of it, remains richly individual and, in all that essentially matters, entirely distinctive from Herbert's. Certainly the two writers can be regarded as true poetic twins; but, like Coleridge and Wordsworth, they are twins of the dissimilar type. With one or two unimportant exceptions, the younger does not imitate the elder. As Mrs Joan Bennett neatly put it : 'Herbert may have made Vaughan a poet, but he did not make him in his own image.'[2]

[1] W Lewis Bettany in his Introduction (p. xxxvii) writes : 'Sometimes, as in *The Tempest*, *The Palm Tree*, and in two stanzas of *Man*, he transmutes Herbert's commoner metals and returns χρυσεα χαλκεων, but more often he gives a poorer replica.' Again, to quote a more modern critic, R. G. Cox states that where Herbert's influence is strongest 'Vaughan usually suffers by the comparison; the effect is thinner and less concentrated' (*From Donne to Marvell*, p. 58).

[2] *Four Metaphysical Poets*, p. 85.

CHAPTER IV

HERMETIC PHILOSOPHY

[The philosopher's stone] is also denominated Silex.
Hermetic Museum, l. 186

THOUGH it was soon to disappear underground, hermeticism (or alchemy) was still a cultural stream of some importance during most of Vaughan's life-time. Its philosophical and religious ideas derived, through some of the main courses of medieval thought, from ultimate sources in neo-platonism and the Cabbala; and, as Miss Elizabeth Holmes rightly says, these ideas 'were of a nature to appeal to that special kind of medievalism which lingered on in Europe till past the first half of the seventeenth century'.[1] On the other hand, its traditional investigation (of a sort) into Nature and its laboratory experimentation certainly led the way towards modern chemistry.

Nothing in Vaughan's poetry has been more exhaustively discussed[2] than its relation to hermeticism, and for that reason the present chapter may be kept relatively short. But the subject is far too important to be ignored altogether.

How far Vaughan's interest in hermeticism sprang from the enthusiasm of his twin-brother, Thomas, who was its leading British exponent, it is hard to say. The brothers were in fairly close contact with each other, and almost all the hermetic ideas to be found in *Silex Scintillans* could have been picked up from conversation with Thomas or from his books. There is no doubt that Henry Vaughan did read his brother's treatises, for his poems contain several clear echoes from them. For example, some of the opening lines of *Cock-Crowing*—

---

[1] *Henry Vaughan and the Hermetic Philosophy*, p. 27.
[2] Besides Miss Holmes' book, the chapter on Vaughan in Miss Mahood's *Poetry and Humanism* is to be specially commended.

Father of lights! what sunny seed,
What glance of day hast thou confin'd
Into this bird? . . .
Their little grain, expelling night . . . .

—unquestionably derive from a sentence in *Anima Magica Abscondita*: 'for she [the soul] is guided in her operations by a spiritual, metaphysical grain, a seed or glance of light . . . descending from the first Father of Lights.'[1] However, there are definite indications in Vaughan's prose-writings of an independent reading of some of the main hermetic authors like Cornelius Agrippa, Paracelsus, and possibly Boehme; and while his hermetic ideas and beliefs owed much to his brother's, they are by no means identical with them. Just to mention one point, he would never have subscribed to Thomas's extreme tenet that 'To speak . . . of God without Nature is more than we can do, for we have not known him so'.[2]

How far did this period of intense interest in hermeticism, which appears to have coincided approximately with the composition of *Silex Scintillans*,[3] affect his poetry?

To make the smallest claim, it certainly gave his poetic vocabulary an unmistakable and individual tinge through such words as *beam, balm, balsam, commerce, essence, exhalation, glance, grain, hatch, influence, invisible* (and *visible*), *key, magnetism, ray, refine, seed, sympathy, tie, veil, vital,* etc. On the whole, this terminology does not clutter his poems with dead learning, and to-day we may take it as a pleasing idiosyncracy rather than a difficulty or obscurity. It is sparingly used, and its terms commonly have some familiar synonym, or else their special meaning is clearly evident from the context. On the other hand, if we

[1] Waite's ed. of Thomas Vaughan, p. 81. The 'house of light' and the 'candle' that is 'tinn'd' are also borrowed from Thomas Vaughan.

[2] Waite's ed., *Euphrates*, p. 395. Elizabeth Holmes comments (*op. cit.*, p. 16): 'Henry's interpretation is finer, less credulous perhaps on some points, but more religious; and here again not only because the Hermetic tradition met the Catholic, and deepened it, and was in its turn refined; but because between them and enriching both lies some individual experience of the poet.'

[3] Hermetic references in *Poems* and *Olor Iscanus* are comparatively few and usually indistinguishable from microcosmism and the general medieval world-picture.

know nothing of hermeticism, we shall sometimes miss certain overtones of Vaughan's language. For instance, the words 'green' and 'greenness', which he was so fond of, not only indicate his peculiar sensitivity to growing things : they also refer to that *benedicta viriditas* that was for the alchemists the essence— and wonder—of the vegetable world.[1] Again, when he describes Christ and his crucifixion as a '*Balsam* of souls' (*The Search*, l. 44), he is not speaking loosely of the comforting power of Christ; 'balsam', as the italics show, was a technical term from hermetic medicine, meaning a preservative in the body that keeps a healthy balance among its elements.[2]

However, Vaughan's poetry owes more to his hermetic reading than a group of somewhat technical words that he uses sporadically, often in isolation, and with the minimum of specialised ideological meaning. He also drew substantially on hermetic thought, to such an extent that most of its main ideas could be readily illustrated from numerous passages in *Silex Scintillans*.

This ideological, as distinct from predominantly verbal, debt does create certain difficulties for the modern reader. For one thing, Vaughan does not always signpost his hermetic references and allusions with an obvious terminology, and for that reason it is sometimes possible to miss them.

An important and revealing example of this difficulty occurs in the last section of *The Waterfall* (a poem that is much less simple and straightforward than it is commonly assumed to be). When we read the lines,

[1] Harold Fisch (*Alchemy and English Literature, Proceedings of the Leeds Philosophical and Literary Society*, Oct. 1953, p. 134) provides an illuminating account of this hermetic significance of green colour: 'Of all colours, it was the colour Green which, in the vegetable world at least, was of utmost importance to the alchemists; if the creative spirit had descended into the mineral world in the form of Mercury it had descended into the vegetable world in the form of greenness. So we find Arthur Dee remarking,

"For when he inspired in things Created, the Generation of the world . . . he gave also a certain Springing and Budding, [that is greenness or strength] . . . and that Greenness they called Nature" (Chymical Collections, 1650. From Preface, *To the Reader*).'

[2] See Vaughan's translation of Nollius' *Hermetical Physick, Works*, p. 551.

Unless that Spirit lead his mind,
Which first upon thy face did move
And hatch'd all with His quick'ning love,

the word 'hatch'd' points fairly clearly to a special hermetic
reference : the alchemists often spoke of the process for producing their stone as a 'hatching', and in this interesting blend of
Christian and hermetic ideas Vaughan is introducing into his
quotation from Genesis 1. 2 the hermetic belief that the world
was created by some kind of 'sacred incubation'.[1]

But how do we take the opening apostrophe of the paragraph ?—

O useful element and clear. . . .

Certainly there is every excuse for the reader dismissing this
line as yet another instance of Vaughan's loose writing, especially in perfunctory rhyme-tagging. Yet the epithet 'useful', so
flat to us to-day, may very well indicate the special hermetical
stress on the part played by water in the cosmic process, as it is
expounded, for instance, by Thomas Vaughan in *Euphrates* :
'This element is the deferent or *vehiculum* of all influences whatsoever. For what efflux soever it be that proceeds from the terrestial centre the same ascends and is carried up in her to the
air. And on the contrary all that comes from heaven descends in
her to the earth, for in her belly the inferior and superior
natures meet and mingle, nor can they be manifested without a
singular artifice.'[2]

If, as seems quite possible, Vaughan intended some such reference as this in his phrase 'useful element', the poem gains not
only in precision but in richness and in closeness of integration.
In the first place, there would be a direct and clear development

---

[1] In *Magia Adamica* (Waite's ed., p. 130) Thomas Vaughan writes : 'the Holy
Spirit, moving upon the chaos—which action some divines compare to the incubation of a hen upon her eggs, did together with his heat consummate other manifold
influences to the matter'; and Sir Thomas Browne has a similar allusion in *Religio
Medici* (xxxii) to 'that gentle heat that brooded on the waters and in six days
hatched the world'. On the other hand, this fusion of Christian and hermetic
notions may have been given to Vaughan, for the reference in the Vulgate, which
keeps close to the original Hebrew verb, reads : 'Spiritus Domini *incubabat* aquis.'

[2] Waite's ed., p. 417.

from the terrestial activity of water, the theme of the previous paragraph, to its cosmic activity, which is taken up again in the later reference to the Creation. In the second place, a delicate pattern of further analogy would be established. As water is the 'vehiculum' of the major physical processes in the cosmos, so through the sacrament of baptism (the subject of the following lines) it is the vehiculum of spiritual development—of divine descent and human ascent.

The same passage from *Euphrates* may also justify Vaughan's apparently casual rhyme. Thomas Vaughan continues: 'Hence it is that whatsoever is pure in the earth, all that she receives from water';[1] and a few pages later he adds: 'certainly by Water and Spirit we must all be regenerated, which made some learned divines affirm that the element of water was not cursed but only that of earth.'[2] If 'clear' was intended to bear some hermetic suggestion of this kind, Vaughan's analogy would take on another facet, water being represented as both a cosmic and spiritual purifier.

With a poet as allusive and suggestive as Vaughan there is also the opposite danger of reading into his work hermetic references where none really exist. For instance, in his article *Hermetic Symbolism in Henry Vaughan's 'The Night'*,[3] Mr B. T. Stewart traces the lines,

> When my Lord's head is fill'd with dew, and all
> His locks are wet with the clear drops of night,

to a passage on the Macroprosopus and the Microprosopus (the revealed countenance of God) in the hermetic work, *The Greater Holy Assembly*:

From the skull of his [the revealed Macroprosopus] head hang down a thousand and five hundred curling hairs, white and pure, like as wool when it is pure. . . .

And in all the hairs is a fountain, which issueth from the hidden brain behind the wall of the skull.

---

[1] Waite's ed., p. 417.   [2] Waite's ed., p. 419.
[3] *Philological Quarterly*, vol. xxix, no. 4, Oct. 1950, pp. 417–21.

And it shineth and goeth forth through that hair unto the hair of the Microprosopus. . . .

In that skull distilleth the dew from the White Head, which is ever filled therewith; and from that dew are the dead raised to life.

On the surface the parallel is a fascinating one and would seem to justify Mr Stewart's comment: 'Henry Vaughan's "dew" and "clear drops of night" are equivalent to this saving dew which springs from the hidden nature of God and flows into the hair of the revealed countenance.' But there is one decisive objection to this alleged source: Vaughan's lines happen to be a quotation, with every word accounted for in *The Song of Songs* 5. 2.[1]

A further difficulty of interpretation arises from the fact that even when Vaughan is certainly evoking hermetical ideas it is not always easy to decide how seriously he is entertaining them. For instance, he commonly describes spiritual shaping and discipline in terms of the purification and refining of metals, as in the following lines from *White Sunday*:

> We, who are nothing but foul clay,
>   Shall be fine gold, which Thou didst cleanse.

> O come! refine us with Thy fire!
>   Refine us! we are at a loss.

No doubt these recurrent metaphors of refining owe something to Malachi 3. 2, but (in another close fusion of Christian and hermetic ideas) they also point unmistakably to a central hermetic belief—the close correspondence, almost identity, between transmutation of the metals and spiritual purification and regeneration, between the alchemic furnaces and the 'furnaces'

---

[1] Mr Stewart, in his attempt to show that *The Night* is filled with 'very rich Hermetic associations', sees the poem as a reaching out beyond the revealed God in Christ towards the dark, unknowable, ultimate Godhead—in hermetic terms, from the Bright Aleph to the Dark Aleph or En Soph. He proves that Thomas Vaughan was familiar with these hermetic conceptions; and it may be that Henry knew of them as well. But the latter part of the poem does not, as Mr Stewart argues, emphasise darkness as symbolic of the unknowable divine nature; stanzas 5–8 treat of night as a time of intimate communion with a knowable God. And there are very strong objections to other alchemic hermetic details of Mr Stewart's interpretation.

of affliction. There can be little question that Thomas Vaughan wholeheartedly believed in this doctrine that 'salvation itself is nothing else but transmutation',[1] which is prominent in his writings; but with Henry it is difficult to decide whether the notion merely furnished an effective poetic metaphor or whether it contributed something of consequence to his own very strong convictions about the value of spiritual suffering.

However, it is likely that the chief effect of hermetic ideas on Vaughan's writing is to be found not in the substance of particular poems but in his general attitude to poetry and its subject matter.

It is wrong to think, as some writers have suggested, that his regeneration intensified and gave a new, central significance to his interest in Nature. On the contrary, there was much in his attitude that might have turned him away from Nature altogether. He held to the doctrine (also found in some of the hermetic writers) that all the Creation was corrupted by the Fall;[2] he shared the common seventeenth-century belief that the end of the world was imminent;[3] and, tortured by a profound sense of the frustration and exile of human life, filled with yearning for the glory and revelation of heaven, he longed continuously, and with utter sincerity, to have done with

> these skies,
> These narrow skies, narrow to me, that bar,
> So bar me in that I am still at war,
> At constant war with them.

Love-Sick

R. H. Walters is if anything understating the point when he says that Vaughan's 'tendency to follow the Christian mystics, and advocate the thwarting of the senses and the shunning of the

---

[1] *Lumen de Lumine,* Waite's ed., p. 302.

[2] See, for example, *Corruption,* ll. 13–16. Cf. Thomas Vaughan, *Anthroposophia Theomagica* (Waite's ed., p. 45) : 'The curse followed, and the impure seeds were joined with the pure, and they reign to this hour in our bodies; and not in us alone but in every other natural thing.'

[3] See *The Jews,* and *Man in Darkness, Works,* p .171.

created world, never exactly fuses with regard for Nature';[1] and we shall never begin to understand Vaughan's attitude to Nature unless we appreciate that it was the very antithesis of the Romantic, and modern, attachment that Charles Lamb has memorably expressed for us: 'I care not to be carried with the tide, that smoothly bears human life to eternity; and reluct at the inevitable course of destiny. I am in love with this green earth; the face of town and country; the unspeakable rural solitudes, and the sweet security of streets. I would set up my tabernacle here.'[2] Indeed, there are moments in *Silex Scintillans* when Vaughan does turn away from Nature, as in *The Search*, with its central theme that God is to be found within:

> Leave, leave thy gadding thoughts;
> Who pores
> And spies
> Still out of doors,
> Descries
> Within them nought.

> The skin and shell of things,
> Though fair,
> Are not
> Thy wish, nor pray'r,
> But got
> By mere despair
> Of wings.

Hermeticism laid an exceptional stress on the religious and poetic significance of the creation, on its richness, wonder, and mystery; and its chief effect on Vaughan's poetry was almost certainly that at the time of his regeneration it acted as the decisive counter-force against those tendencies in him that might have dismissed Nature as 'mere stage and show'. Thanks to his hermetic studies, he was prepared as a Christian poet to

[1] 'Henry Vaughan and the Alchemists', *R.E.S.*, vol. XXIII, no. 90, April 1947, p. 121. Cf. Harold Fisch (*loc. cit.*, p. 130): 'the problem of how to relate their strong religious instincts with a strong and spontaneous delight in Nature was a difficult one for the Christian writers of the period.'

[2] 'New Year's Eve.'

accept, and act upon, his brother's creed: 'In summer translate thyself to the fields, where all are green with the breath of God and fresh with the powers of heaven. Learn to refer all naturals to their spirituals by way of secret analogy. . . . Sometimes thou mayst walk in groves, which being full of mystery will much advance the soul; sometimes by clear active rivers, for by such— say the mystic poets—Apollo contemplated. . . . This is the way I would have thee walk in if thou dost intend to be a solid Christian philosopher.'[1] Here, in words like these, was a lyrical appeal for the 'skin and shell of things' that the poet, if not the man of religion, would find it hard to resist.

There is one poem, 'I walk'd the other day', that in its final and most general section expresses the reconciliation of these divergent attitudes to Nature with particular clarity and conviction. This section begins with an unmistakable hermetic description of the Creation, of the Divine creative fire and the 'hatching' of the world:

> O Thou! whose Spirit did at first inflame
> And warm the dead,
> And by a sacred incubation fed
> With life this frame,
> Which once had neither being, form, nor name;

and a little later there is a compact affirmation of the central hermetic doctrine of God's immanence in Nature—'Who art in all things, though invisibly.' Because God has created Nature and continuously permeates it, Vaughan prays that he may recognise and spiritually profit from the manifestation of God's working:

> Grant I may so
> Thy steps track here below,
>
> That in these masques and shadows I may see
> Thy sacred way;
> And by those hid ascents[2] climb to that day
> Which breaks from Thee,
> Who art in all things, though invisibly.

---

[1] *Anima Magica Abscondita*, Waite's ed., pp. 115–17.

[2] 'Ascents' (the word has an hermetic significance, in the ladder of being) refers to forms of Nature, as in *The Tempest*, l. 37—'All have their keys, and set ascents.'

Further, the first part of the lyric has been a poetic demonstration of this faith, for his meditation on the roots of a plant has led him to a triumphant re-affirmation of his belief in resurrection[1] and to solacing reflections on his dead brother, though (reminding us of his century's indifference to the spiritual significance of Nature) he has to admit

> how few believe such doctrine springs
> From a poor root.

On the other hand, he still regards Nature as 'masques and shadows', part of the life of 'dreams and sorrows' from which he longs to be released; and the poem ends on a note that is the complete opposite of Lamb's :

> And from this care,[2] where dreams and sorrows reign,
> Lead me above,
> Where light, joy, leisure, and true comforts move
> Without all pain.

In this poem—as generally—hermeticism has sustained Vaughan's serious attention to Nature. But his attitude to Nature was a complex and often contradictory one, and there were moments, apparently, when he felt that even the hermetic approach was an unsatisfying and merely transitory phase of spiritual experience, as we may see in *Vanity of Spirit* :

> I summon'd Nature; pierced through all her store;
> Broke up some seals, which none had touched before;
> Her womb, her bosom, and her head,
> Where all her secrets lay abed,
> I rifled quite; and having past
> Through all the creatures, came at last
> To search myself.

[1] The meaning of the lines in stanza 5,
> And stung with fear
> Of my own frailty, dropp'd down many a tear
> Upon his bed,
is a little obscure. Read with the last line of the stanza, 'frailty' cannot mean 'mortal nature'. In general we may perhaps take Vaughan to be expressing a pang of conscience ('stung') that he can ever have doubted, or required a natural proof for, the Christian doctrine of resurrection. 'Fear' remains a difficult word to gloss.

[2] In the light of a general similarity between this stanza and the last stanza of *The World*, might 'care' be a misprint for 'cave', with similar Platonic reference?

Of the main hermetic ideas that figure in *Silex Scintillans* one of the most prominent is certainly that of God perpetually at work in Nature—a conception that Thomas Vaughan presents in such statements as : 'God, like a wise Architect, sits in the centre of all, repairs the ruins of His building, composeth all disorders, and continues his creature in his first primitive harmony.'[1] No doubt, as Hutchinson argues,[2] the doctrine of the Divine immanence in Nature was common enough in traditional Christian writing; but it received little attention from orthodox religious teachers and writers in the seventeenth century, and Vaughan's preoccupation with it must have been stimulated by his hermetic reading. Nor is this just a reasonable supposition, for his expression of the idea is nearly always in specifically hermetic terms, God being represented as generative fire and light, or alternatively as the creative, shaping, moving Spirit of Nature, the *anima mundi*, as in these lines in *Resurrection and Immortality* :

> For a preserving spirit doth still pass
> Untainted through this mass,
> Which doth resolve, produce, and ripen all
> That to it fall.

(In passing, we may note that this first hermetic representation of God's activity in Nature, that of the 'star-fire', ultimately deriving from the Godhead, raying in from the sun and stars, and also present in the Earth and the seeds of the First Matter, partly accounts for the prominence of light imagery in Vaughan's poetry. But, as R. H. Walters has reminded us,[3] this exceptional emphasis on God as fire and light is more a feature of Thomas Vaughan and his acknowledged master, Cornelius Agrippa, than of the hermetists generally.)

Another central hermetic concept that Vaughan continually reflects in *Silex Scintillans* is that of an active relationship of 'sympathy' or 'magnetism' binding together all parts of the creation, especially in the form of a perpetual interaction be-

---

[1] *Anthroposophia Theomagica*, Waite's ed., p. 29.
[2] *Henry Vaughan*, p. 153.
[3] '*Henry Vaughan and the Alchemists*', p. 113.

tween the Divine light and the seeds of star-fire that are in all created things. And here Vaughan's indebtedness to hermeticism is perhaps deeper and more subtle than the specific descriptions of such magnetism that he gives from time to time, in poems like *The Star* and *Cock-Crowing*. What this concept ultimately produces is a singular and unmistakable atmosphere about his poetry, a sense of mysterious activities and influences continuously at work, of integration and harmony—in short, a peculiarly living quality. Miss Elizabeth Holmes has some admirable sentences on this almost indefinable impression : 'Vaughan does more than entertain these [hermetic] beliefs in thought. He lives them in emotion, and then images them in poetry. *The result lies not so much in the frequency of direct reference to Hermetic tradition as in the charging of his poetic atmosphere with this idea of "sympathy"*. Meeting, as we think, some predisposition in himself, it becomes an intuitive knowledge, like an inward sense of touch, directed towards the objects of Nature.'[1]

In discussing this second main hermetic idea that is so prominent in *Silex Scintillans* we have inevitably touched on a third, with which it is inseparably linked. Because they believed that the star-fire, the seeds of the First Matter, and the shaping Divine spirit are everywhere present in Nature, the hermetists drew no sharp demarcation between what we should call 'animate' and 'inanimate' matter : they believed that everything in the creation, including plants and minerals, is essentially living and to some degree sentient. This conception, concentrated in the favourite anthology-piece 'And do they so ?', recurs continually in *Silex Scintillans*, and (a large-scale example of Vaughan's close fusion of hermetic and Christian ideas) it frequently supports his vision of a creation that is for ever praising God and aspiring towards Him.

Besides these continual sources of inspiration, there are many other hermetic ideas that Vaughan draws on from time to time. For example, in lines like

[1] *Op. cit.*, p. 40. My italics.

Thy heav'ns, some say,
Are a fiery-liquid light,[1]

Midnight

or in

Plants in the root with earth do most comply,
Their leaves with water and humidity,
The flowers to air draw near, and subtilty,
And seeds a kindred fire have with the sky,

The Tempest

he is depicting the hermetic view of the cosmos, though admittedly this is a part of hermeticism that is hardly distinct from the medieval and Elizabethan world-picture. Even some of the more incidental alchemic beliefs are reflected occasionally. For instance, the line in *Regeneration*, 'The unthrift Sun shot vital gold,' refers to generation of minerals by the sun—a notion more extensively described in the opening lines of *To I. Morgan* (*Thalia Rediviva*):

So from our cold, rude world, which all things tires,
To his warm Indies the bright sun retires.
Where, in those provinces of gold and spice,
Perfumes his progress, pleasures fill his eyes,
Which, so refresh'd, in their return convey
Fire into rubies, into crystals, day;
And prove, that light in kinder climates can
Work more on senseless stones, than here on man.

But sufficient has been said to establish the considerable importance of Vaughan's hermetic reading for the poetry of *Silex Scintillans*. What remains now is to indicate the limits of this source of inspiration, which has sometimes been over-stressed.

It is certainly true that Vaughan's expression of hermetic ideas sometimes has the prominence—and force—of direct, substantial statement. For example, *The Holy Communion* (a complex expression of the animating, spiritual penetration of matter —of God through the Creation, Christ through man in the Communion, man's soul through his body) contains this direct

[1] See also the whole of the second stanza.

83

and sustained hermetic account of God's continuous interven-
tion in his creation:

> And thus, at first, when things were rude,
> Dark, void, and crude,
> They, by Thy Word, their beauty had and date;
> All were by Thee,
> And still must be;
> Nothing that is, or lives,
> But hath his quick'nings and reprieves,
> As Thy hand opes or shuts;
> Healings and cuts,
> Darkness and daylight, life and death,
> Are but mere leaves turn'd by Thy breath.

On the other hand, at least as many hermetic references—and
probably more—enter his poems in a secondary way: they are
simply convenient material for metaphors, analogies, and illustrations, while often, as we have already said, we cannot be sure
that Vaughan accepts their independent validity.

This leads on to a larger reservation. Though in general Professor Kermode underrates the effect of hermeticism on the
poems of *Silex Scintillans*, he is unquestionably right when he
states that: 'The object of the poet is hardly ever to make the
hermetic or Dionysian idea the central one: it is always illustrative, lighting and enriching the tenuous, often Herbert-
inspired, argument of the poem'.[1] As a poet Vaughan was never
primarily inspired by hermetic beliefs and ideas, and he owed
less to hermeticism than he did to Herbert or the Bible. This is
true even of that small group of lyrics (with *Cock-Crowing* and
The Star as outstanding examples) where hermetic conceptions
have furnished an exceptionally powerful initial impulse that
persists throughout the poem.

Again—with a few exceptions—his best poems are among
the ones that show a minimum of hermetic influence.

Finally, we may speak, truly enough, of the strong hermetic
colouring of his 'picture of Nature'. But when we use descrip-

---

[1] 'The Private Imagery of Henry Vaughan', *R.E.S.*, New Series, vol. 1, no. 3,
p. 214.

tions of this kind we are making an abstraction, and talking about effects rather than causes. From the body of his poetry, with a passage from this lyric and a passage from another, we can certainly build up for ourselves a picture of Nature, just as we can, in the same manner, construct a model of main hermetic doctrine. But in the particular poems, as distinct from the poetry, Vaughan is rarely, if ever, intent on communicating a vision of Nature, hermetic or otherwise. His main concern and inspiration is the relationship between his soul and God, especially in a period of regeneration, that hermeticism might marginally illuminate but could never centrally irradiate or determine.

CHAPTER V

THE BOOK OF NATURE

Translate thyself to the fields. . . .
Anima Magica Abscondita

THE Usk valley, from Brecon, past Newton, where Vaughan lived, to Llansantffraed, where he lies buried, still remains a singularly beautiful stretch of countryside. More than that, richly varied in prospect and bounded for the most part by high hills, though not too narrowly, it creates that unmistakable impression that some localities leave of being a small, self-contained, distinctive world of its own—one that deserves its tutelary poet or painter.

As Vaughan had hoped, in his early poem, *To the River Isca*, he has become that tutelary spirit. All the same it must be said that certain writers have made far too much of him as a poet of Nature; and we have only to compare *The Timber* with two poems that its opening lines readily call to mind, Cowper's *Poplar Field* and Hopkins' *Binsey Poplars*, to appreciate how relatively small was the inspiration of country sights and sounds even for that small group of lyrics in *Silex Scintillans* that may be loosely termed 'Nature poems'. Certainly *The Timber* starts with a fine descriptive passage—and one that was most likely prompted by the actual sight of some fallen tree :

> Sure thou didst flourish once! and many Springs,
>   Many bright mornings, much dew, many showers
> Pass'd o'er thy head; many light hearts and wings,
>   Which now are dead, lodg'd in thy living bowers.
>
> And still a new succession sings and flies;
>   Fresh groves grow up, and their green branches shoot
> Towards the old and still enduring skies,
>   While the low violet thrives at their root.

These two stanzas (two out of fourteen) also lead on to the establishment of one side of an analogy—the fanciful notion of timber that is dead but continues to respond to the approach of storms. However, all this is merely introductory and illustrative matter, for the heart of the poem, which deals with mortification, sin, and repentance, is a meditation on the text: 'He that is dead, is freed from sin' (Rom. 6. 7). It was these words that furnished the primary and essential inspiration of the poem, whereas in *Poplar Field* and *Binsey Poplars* (both of which are far richer than *The Timber* in descriptive detail) the reflections of Cowper and Hopkins arise from the scene they present.

One of the best of Vaughan's Nature poems begins,

> I walk'd the other day, to spend my hour,
> Into a field;

another (less distinguished) with the lines:

> Quite spent with thoughts, I left my cell, and lay
> Where a shrill spring tun'd to the early day;
>
> *Vanity of Spirit*

and there are several poems suggesting that he followed his brother's rule for religious and poetic contemplation.[1] But even in the few poems that have been directly inspired by something he has observed when he has translated himself to the fields, extensive descriptions, like the opening of *The Timber*, are very rare, and the fact is that Nature enters his lyrics chiefly through metaphor and illustration. On the other hand, these images drawn from Nature are sufficiently numerous to leave us, from the body of his poetry, with the clear impression of a distinctive landscape—one of frequent groves and bowers, hillsides and 'clear heights', lively waterfalls and 'restless, vocal' streams that are often mountain-sprung and liable to flood, and of mists, clouds, showers, and broken sunlight.

This landscape is unmistakably the Usk valley below the Brecon Beacons and Alt yr Esgair, and that is why the country-side that was Vaughan's environment for all but a few years of

---

[1] See p. 79.

his life must be set among the most important influences that went to the making of *Silex Scintillans*. Miss Elizabeth Holmes is for once quite wide of the mark when she states that he 'presents a Nature *sub specie aeternitatis*, almost without a local habitation'.[1] At the same time the picture of Nature that his poetry calls up is a highly idealised one—a 'dream' as Blunden rightly describes it.[2] For one thing, as we have already seen, there is the continual overlay of curious hermetic notions and of Biblical landscape. For another, there is the pervasive impression of Spring and Summer, often in the dew-fresh hour of early morning—an Eden ideal, so to speak, that is perfectly captured by such a passage as the following lines from *Ascension Day*:

> I walk the fields of Bethany, which shine
> All now as fresh as Eden, and as fine.
> Such was the bright world, on the first seventh day,
> Before man brought forth sin, and sin decay;
> When like a virgin, clad in flowers and green,
> The pure Earth sat; and the fair woods had seen
> No frost, but flourish'd in that youthful vest,
> With which their great Creator had them dress'd;
> When heav'n above them shin'd like molten glass,
> While all the planets did unclouded pass;
> When springs, like dissolv'd pearls, their streams did pour,
> Ne'er marr'd with floods, nor anger'd with a show'r.

Again, though we encounter an occasional description of the havoc of flood, a phrase as suggestive (though borrowed) as 'howling deserts',[3] or an odd line like

> Though hawks can prey through storms and winds,
> > *The Seed Growing Secretly*

Vaughan has very little regard for the wilder aspects of Nature, in its creatures, landscapes, or elements. He has scarcely

---

[1] *Henry Vaughan and the Hermetic Philosophy*, p. 9.

[2] *On the Poetry of Henry Vaughan*, p. 41. For the same reason Blunden's comparison of Vaughan's descriptions with Claude's paintings has much to commend it. Elizabeth Holmes makes much the same observation when she writes (*op. cit.*, p. 49) that Vaughan's world 'is made up of outward vision and of the dream directing it'.

[3] *Providence*, l. 27. The phrase is almost certainly an echo of Deut. 32. 10.

anything to say of the sea; nor, in spite of the lines in *Ad Posteros*,

> Cambria me genuit, patulis ubi vallibus errans
> Subjacet aeriis montibus Isca pater,[1]

in spite of the hills that everywhere rise in his prospect of earth and heaven, does he ever evoke the Welsh mountain scenery that he must have known well. In all this he was a child of his time, not a precursor of Romantic sensibility.

Little more need be said about his picture of Nature except to add that he had some eye for the creatures—for birds, sheep, mules, asses, moles, glow-worms, and especially bees—and that, like most seventeenth-century poets, he did not treat Nature as synonymous with the countryside. Habitually, not sporadically, his survey took in the whole of man's natural environment—from the stars above to the seeds, roots, and minerals within the earth:

> I in a thought could go
> To Heav'n, or Earth below
> To read some star, or min'ral.
>   *Resurrection and Immortality*

Just as the prominence of Nature in Vaughan's poetry has often been overstressed so his attitude to it has frequently been distorted. And both of these interpretative errors usually arise through the temptation to bring his work into line with Romantic and post-Romantic ways of thought—in particular to treat him as a forerunner of Wordsworth.

No one would quarrel with E. W. Williamson's recent comment that, in contrast with most seventeenth-century poetry, *Silex Scintillans* echoes with notes of a 'genuine countryman'.[2] Only a country poet, familiarly observant of Nature, would think of such an apt and suggestive simile for the awed submission of the Israelites to God as

---

[1] Edmund Blunden's translation:
>   from Wales I drew
> My life, and first its airy mountains knew,
> And Usk below them winding.

[2] *Henry Vaughan*, p. 17.

Thy chosen flock, like leaves in a high wind,
Whisper'd obedience.

The Law and the Gospel

Here is a vivid, first-hand observation that is clearly distinct from the literary (though equally effective) inspiration of

Thick as autumnal leaves that strow the brooks
In Vallombrosa.

Paradise Lost, I. 302-3

Again, to instance a different kind of example, there is no missing the weather-wise countryman, who, in the middle of an entirely religious poem, strikes out the lines,

Those blasts, which o'er our heads here stray,
If showers then fall, will showers allay.

Jesus Weeping II[1]

We also have the interesting testimony of Aubrey, who, unappreciative or ignorant of Vaughan's achievements as a poet, had no doubts about his qualifications as a naturalist. Towards the end of Vaughan's life, when there was apparently some possibility of his collaborating with Dr Plott of Oxford in a work of natural history, Aubrey wrote: '[I] am now sending to my cosn, Henry Vaughan (Silurist) in Brecknockshire to send me the natural history of it, as also of the other circumjacent counties: no man fitter.'[2]

However, countryman as Vaughan was, enlivening his verse with touches of first-hand observation and rarely bookish in the descriptive manner of so many of his contemporaries, he certainly cannot be regarded as a precursor of that diverse band of poets, from Wordsworth to Andrew Young, who in the last

[1] For another countryman's poem see *De Salmone*, also excellently translated by Blunden.

[2] Quoted Footnote 1, p. xlii, in the *Muses Library* ed. of Vaughan's poems. Nothing came of this project. But Vaughan was certainly interested in it and evidently considered himself suitably qualified for the task proposed. He almost sounds like a seventeenth-century Gilbert White when he informs Aubrey: 'If in my attendance upon (rather than speculations into) Nature, I can meet with anything that may deserve the notice of that learned and Honourable Society, I shall humbly present you with it, and leave it wholly to your censure and disposal' (*Works*, p. 672). (See Letters III and IV in *Works*, pp. 671-2.)

hundred and fifty years have found so much poetic stimulation in
the close study of Nature and in the challenge of communicating
their observations in exact but evocative language. Whatever
may have been his interests in everyday, and especially later,
life, and even though he talks of himself as one who had 'unbowel'd nature',[1] he was not to any important extent a naturalist when he was writing his poetry. As Williamson himself
admits, 'in [Vaughan's] poems there is not much minute
observation'.[2]

Besides the naturalist's interest, Romantic and post-Romantic
poetry has also been marked by a vital aesthetic response to
Nature, and something of this is present too in the poems of
Silex Scintillans. Vaughan's main Nature images and symbols—
his dews, streams, stars, and so on—are rarely mere counters,
while at all times his abiding dream of heaven is coloured, however paradoxically, by some love for the sights and sounds of
earth, so that even when he is writing about his memory of the
happy dead, 'all gone into the world of light,' he will characteristically illustrate his feelings by a simile that simultaneously
reveals the keenest appreciation of terrestial beauty :

> It glows and glitters in my cloudy breast,
>> Like stars upon some gloomy grove,
> Or those faint beams in which this hill is dress'd,
>> After the sun's remove.

On the other hand, though a number of short passages like this
may be gathered from his poetry, on the whole his painting of
Nature is neither rich nor particularly stimulating in sensuous
impression. To appreciate his limitations there is hardly any
need to set his picture of hills in the last light of the setting sun
against the Romantic Housman's more vivid and deeply felt
lines :

---

[1] In this, and one or two similar references, Vaughan is probably referring to his
hermetic studies. R. H. Walters, however, interprets : 'When Vaughan "unbowel'd
nature", he was seeking moral lessons, parables for man's spiritual welfare'
(*Vaughan and the Alchemists*, p. 121).
[2] *Op. cit.*, p. 17.

> Wenlock Edge was umbered,
>   And bright was Abdon Burf,
> And warm between them slumbered
>   The smooth green miles of turf;
> Until from grass and clover
>   The upshot beam would fade,
> And England over
>   Advanced the lofty shade.[1]

Even when we measure his writing against some of the Nature descriptions of his own century—those in Marvell's *The Garden*, for instance, or in Milton's *Lycidas*, *Comus*, or Book IV of *Paradise Lost*—its lack of sensuous vitality is plain enough.

Once at least, in *Cock-Crowing*, he seems to have glimpsed the way of reconciling full sensuous delight in the physical beauty of Nature with an awareness of the Divine glory manifest in that beauty, the way of Hopkins and, so far as he was concerned with Nature, of Crashaw :

> O Thou immortal light and heat!
> Whose hand so shines through all this frame,
> That by the beauty of the seat,
> We plainly see Who made the same.

But this was never his settled attitude, and when we read some of his earlier poems like *Fida: Or the Country-beauty*, with its surprisingly Keatsian relish in the experience of the senses, we cannot help feeling that his regeneration, besides raising profound doubts about the significance of Nature, also led him to repress, or at least drastically restrain, a lively sensuous responsiveness. Perhaps some lines in *The Hidden Treasure*, though their main reference seems to be to sexual love, point to the same conclusion :

> Man's favourite sins, those tainting appetites,
> Which Nature breeds, and some fine clay invites,
> With all their soft, kind arts and easy strains,
> Which strongly operate, though without pains,
> Did not a greater beauty rule mine eyes,
> None would more dote on, nor so soon entice.

[1] *Fancy's Knell.*

Finally, in clearing the ground of some common misconceptions about Vaughan's attitude, we must entirely separate his (mainly hermetic) conception of the Divine in Nature from Wordsworth's pantheism and belief in the possibility of spiritual communion through the medium of Nature. Whatever certain good critics may have said to the contrary,[1] and in spite of some intense images of identification with Nature—a different matter —there is nothing in Vaughan's poetry that remotely resembles the sort of mystical communion that Wordsworth records in such a passage as

> And I have felt
> A presence that disturbs me with the joy
> Of elevated thoughts : a sense sublime
> Of something far more deeply interfused,
> Whose dwelling is the light of setting suns,
> And the round ocean and the living air,
> And the blue sky, and in the mind of man :
> A motion and a spirit, that impels
> All thinking things, all objects of all thought,
> And rolls through all things.[2]

Itrat-Husain has admirably, and without exaggeration, stated the essential difference between these two poets whose attitudes to Nature are so frequently confused : 'Vaughan is no Nature mystic like Wordsworth, for he realised that he could only apprehend God through the grace of Christ, and that, after having recognised the glory and grandeur of the created universe, one has to seal one's eyes to it.'[3]

For Vaughan, following hermetic doctrine and to some extent

---

[1] G. Williamson (*The Donne Tradition*, p. 132) writes that 'Nature speaks to him in pantheistic terms that anticipate Wordsworth'. Mrs Joan Bennett (*Four Metaphysical Poets*, p. 88) describes Vaughan as a poet 'who resembles Wordsworth in his nature mysticism'; and Elizabeth Holmes states that Vaughan 'seeks to merge himself and be lost in the midst of the natural scene' (*op. cit.*, p. 10). With these comments compare R. H. Walters (*loc. cit.*, p. 121) : 'Unlike Wordsworth, Vaughan never suggests that it is possible to pass directly from the study of nature to the experience of contact with the divine.'

[2] *Lines composed a few miles above Tintern Abbey*, ll. 94–103.

[3] *The Mystical Element in the Metaphysical Poets of the Seventeenth Century*, p. 212.

emblematic habit, Nature was above all else a 'living Library',[1] a repository of 'lectures' and 'instructions' (for he never eschews such pietistic words); and his attitude is centrally and explicitly stated in *The Tempest* :[2]

> O that man could do so! that he would hear
> The world read to him! all the vast expense
> In the creation shed, and slav'd to sense,
> Makes up but lectures for his eye and ear.

> Sure, Mighty Love, foreseeing the descent
> Of this poor creature, by a gracious art
> Hid in these low things snares to gain his heart
> And laid surprises in each element.

The particular 'lessons' of Nature that he transcribes in his poems are simple, often fanciful and unconvincing, and sometimes reiterated to monotony. 'I walk'd the other day', with its avowal of resurrection, teaches what, in *Man in Darkness*, he maintained to be one of the two primary lessons of the creation —'these prolusions and strong proofs of our restoration laid out in nature' (p. 177). The other outstanding and complementary lesson—'There is no object we can look upon, but will do us the kindness to put us in mind of our mortality' (p. 174)[3]—is most emphatically rehearsed in *The Check* :

> View thy fore-runners : Creatures, giv'n to be
> Thy youth's companions,
> Take their leave, and die : birds, beasts, each tree,
> All that have growth or breath,
> Have one large language, death!

However, the chief stress of the poems, so far as Nature is concerned, falls on two other lessons. The first, and most recurrent of these (central in 'And do they so?', *The Tempest*, *Cock-Crow-*

---

[1] *Anthroposophia Theomagica*, Waite's ed., p. 26—'Man hath the use of all these creatures, God having furnished him with a living Library wherein to employ himself.' The idea of the *Liber Creatorum* is of course older than seventeenth-century hermeticism and independent of it.

[2] See also *Rules and Lessons*, ll. 85–96.

[3] This and the preceding page reference is to L. C. Martin's *Vaughan's Works*.

ing, and *The Bird*) is the intentness of the creatures on God—their watchfulness, their continuous aspiration upwards for reunion with their divine origin, and, above all, their hymns of praise:

> All things that be praise Him; and had
> Their lesson taught them when first made.
>
> *The Bird*

The second (concentrated in *The Constellation* and *Man*) is the obedience, order, and stability of the creatures:

> Weighing the steadfastness and state
> Of some mean things which here below reside,
> Where birds, like watchful clocks, the noiseless date
> And intercourse of times divide,
> Where bees at night get home and hive, and flow'rs
> Early as well as late,
> Rise with the sun and set in the same bow'rs. . . .
>
> *Man*

As in this poem, the virtues of the creatures are usually sharply juxtaposed with the weaknesses and limitations of fallen man[1]—intentness against disregard and sleep, 'steadfastness' against perpetual restlessness and straying. One result of this is that sometimes (as notably in *Man* and *Cock-Crowing*) Vaughan achieves a fine poem through some impressive statement on the human condition and in spite of the fanciful or obvious lesson of Nature that he is presenting. Indeed, by the end of *Cock-Crowing*, apart from a superficial link in 'light' imagery, he has moved far away from his original lesson; and the cock's punctual greeting of the light, the hermetic fancy of some magnetism between the sun and a grain of star-fire in the bird, lead not so much to a plea for watchfulness, prayer, and praise as to a memorable expression of his yearning to break through the veil of the flesh and be united with God.

[1] Cf. S. L. Bethell, *The Cultural Revolution of the Seventeenth Century*, p. 95: 'Vaughan's sympathy is with nature. Fallen man, redeemed yet still far from perfection, is the problem-child of God; all the rest of the universe harmoniously rejoices before Him.'

As a library, Nature is read by him in diverse ways. In some of the poems, such as *The Shower, Midnight, The Storm, The Star, The Waterfall*, it merely serves for analogy and illustration, often in the emblematic manner.[1] Thus in *The Shower* the cycle of stagnant water–exhalations–rain provides metaphors, rather strained ones, for certain linked spiritual states; in *The Star* the 'commerce' between the star and its magnetic earthly object an analogy for the desirable kind of communion between God and the human soul. But in other poems, in 'And do they so?', *The Constellation, Man*, and *The Bird*, for instance, Nature is represented as teaching directly by the good, of a general or specifically religious kind, that Vaughan believes it to manifest. Most of the Nature poems fall into one or the other of these two groups; but because of his reluctance, on hermetic grounds, to admit of anything inanimate in Nature there are one or two poems, like *Cock-Crowing*, in which the distinction breaks down. Again, we find the same object of Nature treated now in one way, now in the other. For instance, there is an obvious difference between the hermetic fancy of

> Some kind herbs here, though low and far,
> Watch for and know their loving star,
>
> *The Favour*

and

> Where trees and herbs did watch and peep
> And wonder, while the Jews did sleep.
>
> *The Night*

Another possible attitude to Nature is that of subjective identification with it. There are only two poems, *Unprofitableness* and *Mount of Olives II*, that are extensively written in this mode; but this identification is fairly common in Vaughan's incidental references to Nature, especially when they form metaphors for some spiritual state.

[1] See Rosemary Freeman, *English Emblem Books*, pp. 149–53. E.g.: 'Both in his habit of handling abstract ideas as if they were tangible and visible objects, and in his way of interpreting phenomena in the natural world which so powerfully impressed him, Vaughan writes in a manner that can be called emblematic' (p. 151).

Though Vaughan's attitude to Nature was undoubtedly shaped chiefly by his hermetic reading, it was also moulded by some important secondary influences—the Bible (especially the *Psalms*), his wide theological reading, the Emblem books, and the poetry of Boethius and Casimirus.

In particular, he may have owed a considerable debt to Casimirus, and there is a passage in his translation of *The Praise of a Religious Life* that adumbrates in a quite remarkable way many of the main ideas and sentiments that occur in *Silex Scintillans* whenever he is writing about Nature. This passage begins with an affirmation of what was to become his central and settled belief: that Nature is an appearance of 'Veils and shades' but none the less worthy of serious contemplation because of its manifestation of God. (It will also be noticed that the season is, characteristically, 'calm Spring') :

> In the calm Spring, when the Earth bears,
> And feeds on April's breath and tears,
> His eyes, accustom'd to the skies,
> Find here fresh objects, and like spies
> Or busy bees, search the soft flow'rs,
> Contemplate the green fields and bow'rs,
> Where he in veils and shades doth see
> The back parts of the Deity. . . .

Shortly after this the poem turns to Vaughan's favourite image of the plants aspiring to heaven, brings in the contrast of earth-centred man, and is rounded off by a typical reference to springs and fountains :

> Then sadly sighing says, 'O! how
> These flow'rs with hasty, stretch'd heads grow
> And strive for heav'n, but rooted here
> Lament the distance with a tear!
> The honeysuckles clad in white,
> The rose in red, point to the light;
> And the lilies, hollow and bleak,
> Look as if they would something speak;
> Then sigh at night to each soft gale,
> And at the day-spring weep it all.
> Shall I then only—wretched I!—

Oppress'd with earth, on earth still lie?'
Thus speaks he to the neighbour trees,
And many sad soliloquies
To springs and fountains doth impart,
Seeking God with a longing heart.

Out of this discussion of Vaughan's inspiration from the countryside in which he lived and wrote, several conclusions plainly emerge. For his moments of first-hand observation and for the significance he attached to Nature in his religious beliefs (these two tendencies often producing an unusual freshness, intensity, and urgency in his imagery) he was exceptional among the poets of the seventeenth century. He walked in the fields; they were the Brecon fields; and in them he saw the continuous handiwork of God. But, granted these distinguishing qualities of his work, he was essentially of his age, not a Romantic born out of his time; and certainly, so far as the extent of his descriptive writing is concerned, he is no more of a Nature poet than Herrick, Milton, Marvell, or Traherne.

Further, it is most unlikely that he would ever have regarded himself, in any notable sense, as a poet of Nature. Nature-poetry demands—among other qualities—a richness and vitality of sensuous response that he never possessed or, more probably, that he curbed and smothered. It also demands a love of earth such as he felt only fugitively and was often inclined to reject altogether.

PART II

STUDIES OF
FOUR MAJOR POEMS

CHAPTER VI

'REGENERATION'—
AN INTERPRETATION

A ward, and still in bonds, one day
  I stole abroad;
It was high-Spring, and all the way
  Primros'd, and hung with shade:
   Yet was it frost within;   5
    And surly winds
Blasted my infant buds, and sin
  Like clouds eclips'd my mind.

Storm'd thus, I straight perceiv'd my Spring
  Mere stage and show;   10
My walk a monstrous, mountain'd thing,
  Rough-cast with rocks, and snow;
   And as a pilgrim's eye,
    Far from relief,
Measures the melancholy sky,   15
  Then drops, and rains for grief:

So sigh'd I upwards still; at last
  'Twixt steps and falls,
I reach'd the pinnacle, where plac'd
  I found a pair of scales;   20
   I took them up, and laid
    In th' one late pains,
The other smoke, and pleasures weigh'd
  But prov'd the heavier grains.

With that, some cried, 'Away'; straight I   25
    Obey'd, and led
Full East, a fair, fresh field could spy;
    Some call'd it, Jacob's Bed;
    A virgin soil, which no
      Rude feet e'er trod;   30
Where—since He stept there—only go
    Prophets, and friends of God.

Here I repos'd; but scarce well set,
    A grove descried
Of stately height, whose branches met   35
    And mix'd, on every side;
    I enter'd, and once in,
      Amaz'd to see 't,
Found all was chang'd, and a new Spring
    Did all my senses greet.   40

The unthrift sun shot vital gold,
    A thousand pieces;
And heaven its azure did unfold
    Chequer'd with snowy fleeces;
    The air was all in spice,   45
      And every bush
A garland wore: thus fed my eyes,
    But all the ear lay hush.

Only a little fountain lent
    Some use for ears,   50
And on the dumb shades language spent
    The music of her tears;
    I drew her near, and found
      The cistern full
Of divers stones, some bright and round,   55
    Others ill-shap'd and dull.

The first, pray mark, as quick as light
  Danc'd through the flood;
But th' last, more heavy than the night,
  Nail'd to the centre stood;   60
  I wonder'd much, but tir'd
    At last with thought,
My restless eye, that still desir'd,
  As strange an object brought.

It was a bank of flowers, where I descried,   65
  Though 'twas mid-day,
Some fast asleep, others broad-eyed,
  And taking in the ray;
  Here musing long, I heard
    A rushing wind,   70
Which still increas'd, but whence it stirr'd,
  Nowhere I could not find.

I turn'd me round, and to each shade
  Dispatch'd an eye,
To see if any leaf had made   75
  Least motion or reply;
  But while I list'ning sought
    My mind to ease
By knowing, where 'twas, or where not,
  It whisper'd, 'Where I please.'   80

'Lord,' then said I, 'on me one breath,
And let me die before my death!'

To examine [*Regeneration*] in detail is a pleasant obligation upon Vaughan's admirers, for it seems to be the definite record of his passing from the circle of wits and revellers into the spiritual world.

E. BLUNDEN, On the Poems of Henry Vaughan (p. 20)

To him that hath designed a superstructure of true blessings the fundamental must be Salvation.   *The World Contemned* (p. 315)

'REGENERATION' lies at the beginning of *Silex Scintillans* somewhat like *The Wreck of the Deutschland* at the beginning of Hopkins' *Poems*—an undoubted major work of its author, filled with his most admirable and characteristic qualities (though narrative in pattern) but, at the same time, a little daunting, especially to the new reader, because of its length, complexity and obscurity.

Of course the difficulties of *Regeneration* are not so great as those of *The Wreck of the Deutschland*, nor are they of the same kind. Unlike Hopkins' poem, *Regeneration* has a beautifully translucent surface, its obscurities arising chiefly from its allegorical intention and its unusual amount of largely private symbolism, those

> hidden, dispers'd truths that folded lie
> In the dark shades of deep allegory.
>
> *Monsieur Gombauld*

Once we have unravelled these allegorical 'truths' the poem is readily accessible, and certainly, following the guidance of its title, its significant position as the opening of *Silex Scintillans*, and the close parallel between its last stanzas and the conclusion of *The World*, we should never be in any serious doubts about its main theme. It is a poetic record of Vaughan's recovery—and in a large sense discovery—of religious faith; of his return to grace and his hope of election. Above all, of his hope of election, which is also seen against the general mystery of election and predestination[1]—the inspiration of God's spirit blowing where it listeth.

[1] The urgency of this theme for a religious poet of Vaughan's time is clearly brought out by H. C. White (*op. cit.*, p. 285) : 'Predestination was at the beginning of the century the official theory of the English Church, but in practice . . . men like Donne had seriously modified it in the direction of free will. The state of mind, however, for which it was of first importance to make sure that one had within himself the immediate and certain confidence of his own salvation, lingered long after intellectual accommodations were pretty widely accepted, and undoubtedly this was reinforced by the conversion and regeneration theories that came to play so large a part in the thought of the more "Enthusiastic" groups of the time.'

Though the first two lines of the poem indicate clearly enough the start of some spiritual journey, in their detail they are rather puzzling. 'In bonds' presumably refers to sin. But if that is the meaning, how are we to reconcile this idea of hateful imprisonment with 'ward', which, used in its common sense, would imply some kind of desirable, protective guardianship? Possibly Vaughan is extending the Old Testament use of 'ward' ('imprisonment', 'the condition of being a prisoner') to mean 'prisoner'. Again, he may be saying that, for all his bondage to sin, he is still under the guardianship of God. This would probably have been an acceptably orthodox point of view. But the expression of the idea through two closely joined but different metaphors would be awkward. And is the spiritual condition (whatever it is) that is described in the first line something that the pilgrim is escaping from or that he takes with him?

The rest of the stanza, which expresses the poet-pilgrim's acutely divided state of being, is quite straightforward. On the surface his life seems to be one of 'high-Spring'—of youth and enjoyed pleasure; but underneath there is the winter of sin and spiritual desolation, in which the divine spark within him is entirely obscured. The description of these two states is linked by a common, and highly characteristic, vegetal imagery, with 'Primros'd' probably carrying the deliberate ambiguity of youth and the path of destruction; and the blighted soul is represented by the typical metaphor of the frost- and wind-ravaged plant. (There is a particularly close parallel to lines 5–7, with a similar context of 'Breaking the link 'Twixt Thee and me', in *Disorder and Frailty*:

> though here tost
> By winds, and bit with frost. . . .)[1]

Further adding to the densely characteristic quality of the first stanza there is also the recurrent image of the eclipsing cloud, with which, as has already been suggested,[2] we may relevantly associate the latent detail of the star and therefore the divine

---

[1] For another parallel, see *Mount of Olives II*, ll. 11–14.   [2] See p. 26.

spark. Certainly, when Vaughan speaks of his 'eclips'd' mind, he is not thinking of his intellectual faculties, but, as the penultimate stanza makes plain, of his soul that, were all well with him, would be open to the Divine 'ray'.

The second stanza records the first advance in the poet's pilgrimage, when, realising his divided condition, he perceives that his 'high-Spring' is an illusion. ('Show', which may echo Psalms 39. 6—'Surely every man walketh in a vain show'—almost certainly carries the double meaning of illusory, external appearance and of spectacle, pageant, etc., while 'stage', besides being synonymously linked with the second meaning of 'show', may also include the sense of 'phase'.) In the only reality that matters the pilgrim's walk is

> a monstrous, mountain'd thing,
> Rough-cast with rocks, and snow

—an image that powerfully concentrates suggestions of appalling alienation from the true and natural order of things ('monstrous'), of something fearsome and even horrible (for that was how mountains seemed to the common sensibility of the time), of sterility, and of impending destruction. This notable advance brings with it, though an overwhelming sense of sin, the temptation of despair.[1] But there is no indication that the pilgrim is seriously troubled by this temptation, unless that is the implication of the phrase "Twixt steps and falls' (l. 18). Even in grief his sighs have been significantly 'upwards', and while it is unlikely that 'pinnacle' bears any special suggestion, the line, 'I reach'd the pinnacle,' clearly implies that, in spite of some suffering and set-back, the poet has struggled to a state above and beyond despair.

At this point there is a momentary halt in the progress of the poem as the pilgrim reflects on the pains of his recent ascent. The focus of this reflection is a discovered 'pair of scales'—a familiar object from the emblem books[2] but treated by Vaughan

---

[1] Ll. 13–16 are somewhat reminiscent of a passage in one of Vaughan's translations from Casimirus—lib. 3, Ode 22, 15–18. The first two lines of this translation might be taken as a summary of the first two stanzas of *Regeneration*.

[2] Rosemary Freeman, *English Emblem Books*, p. 150.

in such a way that it runs into some obscurity of reference—and of syntax. As commonly used, by Quarles for instance, this emblem is simple enough: the scales demonstrate the worthless lightness of the things of the world, etc., balanced against the substantial weight of spiritual things.[1] Vaughan appears to reverse this usage in two ways, for in his treatment of the emblem what is rejected is the heavier side of the scales, and the heavier side is constituted of worldly pleasures, which, with a further complicating paradox, are 'smoke'! However, the main confusion of these lines is created not so much by the reversal of the usual emblem as by Vaughan's adaptation of it to an unsuitable purpose. We may read the passage in one of two ways: in the first, we understand that whereas the 'late pains' carried the poet upwards, to the pinnacle, his worldly 'pleasures' would have borne him down to earth, hell and damnation—to the 'centre' that he speaks of later in the poem; in the second, the 'late pains' are considered as of small consequence against weightily damning pleasures. In the first, Vaughan would be expressing an idea for which his emblem is unsuitable; in the second, he would be violently straining the emblem into a false measurement, since the 'pains' can have no weight, no earthward and hellward tendency, whatsoever.[2]

Sufficient probably to take the lines in the brief and essential paraphrase that all the pilgrim's ordeals, in his ascent to the pinnacle, were of small account against what was to follow.

The voices at the pinnacle, though they may be angelic, are probably of no particular significance, merely a narrative device. But in obeying them and continuing a stage further in his jour-

---

[1] The *Epigram* to Quarles's *A Pair of Balances* (bk. 1 no. IV) reads:
   My soul, what's lighter than a feather? Wind.
   Than wind? The fire. And what, than fire? The mind.
   What's lighter than the mind? A thought. Than thought?
   This bubble world. What than this bubble? Nought.

[2] There is perhaps yet another way of taking this obscure figure: that at this stage in his spiritual development the poet resents the 'pains' of his pilgramage, and that his heart still chiefly values the 'pleasures', even though they are 'smoke'. He has not yet found the true joy of the religious life.

ney, the poet-pilgrim is afforded a revelation of God; and this revelation constitutes the central theme of stanzas 4–6. The 'East' towards which the pilgrim travels symbolises the dawn of light and illumination in general and of the Scriptures, especially perhaps the Old Testament, in particular. The first intimation of communion with the revealed God is given by a straightforward allusion to Jacob's vision of God in a dream before Bethel (Gen. 28. 11 ff.); and this field of revelation is described as 'fresh' and 'virgin' because for each individual soul the moment of illumination comes as an eternally original experience. The last four lines of stanza 4 express a familiar idea in *Silex Scintillans*: that in earliest Old Testament days men enjoyed a particularly close intimacy with God, 'Friends of God' referring explicitly to the patriarchs (James 2. 23).

However, the intimations of communion with God that follow are much more subtle and private and require some knowledge of the whole of Vaughan's poetry for their full appreciation. For instance, the significance of the 'grove' that the pilgrim soul enters (stanza 5) is not likely to be apparent until we understands the peculiar but strong association that existed in Vaughan's imagination between God and groves. Nothing better illuminates this stanza than the opening of *Religion* (a poem printed in the first few pages of *Silex Scintillans* and therefore possibly composed in the same period as *Regeneration*) where Vaughan nostalgically pictures the earliest Old Testament days as a time when man was in familiar, speaking contact with God and his angels under a canopy of trees :

> My God, when I walk in those groves
> And leaves, Thy spirit doth still fan,
> I see in each shade that there grows
> An angel talking with a man, etc.

(It is also interesting to notice, for the parallel, that where the 'grove' stanza in *Regeneration* immediately follows the reference to 'Jacob's Bed', *Religion* also has, shortly after its opening, the line, 'Here Jacob dreams, and wrestles.')

This link between groves and religious experience, especially of communion with God, is certainly a strange one, since a poet who knew his Bible so well as Vaughan must have been thoroughly aware of the recurrent, almost ominous, associations in the Old Testament between groves and pagan worship. Something of its establishment may have been due to the influence of Herbert, for the opening of *Religion* is certainly a reminiscence of Herbert's poem, *Decay* :

> Sweet were the days, when Thou didst lodge with Lot,
> Struggle with Jacob, sit with Gideon. . . .
>
> One might have sought and found Thee presently
> At some fair oak, or bush. . . .

Again, as several writers have suggested, following the note in L. C. Martin's edition, the 'grove' reference in *Regeneration* may be one of several echoes from his brother's treatise, *Lumen de Lumine* : 'Being thus troubled to no purpose, and wearied with long endeavours, I resolved to rest myself, and seeing I could find nothing, I expected if anything could find me. I had not long continued in this humour, but I could hear the whispers of a soft wind that travelled towards me, and suddenly it was in the leaves of the trees, so that I concluded myself to be in some wood, or wilderness.'[1] Later in *Lumen de Lumine* there is the sentence : 'I found myself in a grove of bays.' But along with these possible echoes we must also take into consideration an obvious feature of Vaughan's poetic development in *Silex Scintillans*—his adaptation of images and sensuous delights of his unregenerate days to the 'sacred poems' of his conversion. He had always loved trees and woods and felt something of the mystery of woodland places, as we may see from such early poems as *Upon the Priory Grove* and from passages in *Ad*

---

[1] Waite's ed., pp. 243–4. However, if Vaughan was recollecting this passage, it is surprising that he did not take up the impressive description of light that immediately follows it.

Echum[1] and *To the River Isca,* and it is not difficult to trace the probable source of the 'grove' stanza in such a pagan fancy as

> May vocal groves grow there, and all
> The shades in them prophetical,
> Where laid men shall more fair truths see
> Than fictions were of Thessaly!
>
> *To the River Isca*

Possibly stanza 5 carries yet another implication. This grove

> Of stately height, whose branches met
> And mix'd, on every side,

is also suggestive of the interior of some church or cathedral, with all its columns, pillars, and arches. Whether or not Vaughan deliberately intended this suggestion it is hard to say, but the entry into the grove might, just possibly, signify entrance into church worship. Another pointer (admittedly a slight one) in the direction of this reading is the allusion in the following and closely connected stanza to *The Song of Songs,* a book currently interpreted as celebrating the marriage between Christ and his Church.

The transition from the grove of stanza 5 to the flowery bushes and spicy air of stanza 6 was no doubt chiefly inspired by Vaughan's epigraph from *The Song of Songs* 4. 16—'Arise O North, and come thou South-wind, and blow upon my garden, that the spices thereof may flow out.' This verse, echoed in stanza 6, and, in its allegorical interpretation, a key to the whole poem, was almost certainly running in Vaughan's head right from the start of the composition. At the same time the development may also have been prompted to some extent by a suggestion from *Lumen de Lumine,* for the first passage already quoted

---

[1] See especially the lines (in Edmund Blunden's translation):
> O Nymph, that through the drowsy thicket fliest,
> And boughs beloved, and sauntering there repliest
> Out of the deeps: Spirit of this old grove. . . .
> Show me the mystery of this tangled maze,
> The happy secret of these his green ways,
> Thy home, thy walks!

is followed by : 'With this gentle breath came a most heavenly, odorous air, much like that of sweet briars, but not so rank, and full.'[1]

So far as its meaning is concerned, stanza 6 is certainly another symbolical representation of the pilgrim's experience of the Divine illumination.[2] This interpretation is perhaps sufficiently established by the line,

The unthrift sun shot vital gold,

since the sun here is undoubtedly to be connected with the Divine 'ray' of illumination in stanza 9. Further, with the alchemic reference to the sun's action in generating precious stones and gold, we must also take that hermetic analogy between chemical transmutation and spiritual regeneration that makes the allusion an extremely apt one in its context. But once again a really convincing demonstration of Vaughan's meaning and intention depends on familiarity with the body of his poetry, which, as we have already seen,[3] reveals a very clear connection between scents, occasionally flowers, the sun, and divine visitation.

The echo from *The Song of Songs* suggests another significance in stanza 6 besides the main one of spiritual illumination. Like stanza 5, with which it is so closely linked, it may celebrate the pilgrim's entrance into Christ's Church. And there are several other important implications. 'Vital gold' may also be used for its common symbolical significance of eternal life, its incorruptibility, while the choice of the word 'heaven' for sky[4] and 'snowy' (here probably indicative of purity as 'snow' in stanza 2 is of sterility) might imply a glimpse of the beatitudes

---

[1] It is also to be noticed that stanza 6 contains a word, 'chequer'd', that is rare in Vaughan's vocabulary but occurs in his brother's treatise—'The ground both near and far off presented a pleasing kind of chequer.'

[2] Cf. Thomas Vaughan's *Anima Magica Abscondita,* p. 85 : 'we might enter the Terrestial Paradise, that encompassed the Garden of Solomon, where God descends to walk and drink of the Sealed Fountain.'

[3] See pp. 28–9.

[4] Though there is nothing conclusive in the reference we should perhaps notice the line describing God in heaven in *Retirement*—'Who on yon throne of azure sits', for 'azure' is a rare word in Vaughan's poetic vocabulary.

of the after-life. Again, from the explicit statement at the end of stanza 5, the paradisal garden that Vaughan depicts (one of the most richly sensuous descriptions in the whole of his poetry) is certainly to be taken as an intimation of the 'new spring' that is in contrast with the false spring at the outset of the pilgrim's journey. This strand of meaning is closely woven with another that is of the utmost importance for the development of the poem. This delightful garden of sweet airs and flowering bushes represents, quite simply, the beauty of religion. Just so that other poem of Vaughan's regeneration, *Mount of Olives II*, begins with:

> When first I saw True Beauty....[1]

By this revealed beauty of the religious life the pilgrim's eyes are fed. But he has a stage further to go in his path towards salvation: 'All the ear lay hush'—he has still to receive the word of Christ, and Christ himself. This vital but obscure link in the development of the poem is clearly illuminated by a passage in *The World Contemned*: 'Why with so much dotage do we fix our eyes upon the deceitful looks of temporal things? . . . Is it the Eye alone that we live by? Is there nothing useful about us but that wanderer? We live also by the ear, and at that inlet we receive the glad tidings of Salvation, which fill us with earnest groans for our glorious liberty and the consummation of the promises. . . . That faithful one, the blessed Author of those promises, assures us frequently of his fidelity and performance; let us covet earnestly his best promises.'[2] In *Regeneration* Vaughan is not condemning the eye, nor has he been concerned with its regard for temporal things; but the ear that 'lay hush' is certainly waiting for the 'glad tidings of Salvation' and the 'blessed Author of those promises'.

The 'fountain' image in stanza 7 was probably 'given' to Vaughan at this point in the poem by preceding developments. For one thing, reminiscence of the fourth chapter of *The Song of*

---

[1] There is another passage in *Mount of Olives II* (ll. 17–20) that points straight to stanza 6.

[2] *Works*, p. 326.

Songs during the composition of stanza 6 may very well have stirred an echo of verse 12—'as a Spring shut up, and a fountain sealed up.'[1] Again, the mention of 'Jacob's Bed' in stanza 4 may already have brought into his mind the idea of Jacob's well, the fountain beside which Christ spoke to the woman of Samaria, for he was certainly very familiar with this allusion to Jacob's well in John 4, as we may see from *The Mount of Olives* and his poem *The Search*.[2] Finally, the 'fountain' may have come in direct association with the 'grove' of stanza 5 since there are at least half a dozen instances of this image conjunction in his poetry.[3]

Apart from the clue given us by the passage already quoted from *The World Contemned*, numerous other passages in Vaughan's prose and poetry (in the two *Jesus Weeping* poems, for instance) make it reasonably certain that the 'fountain' in the first part of stanza 7 symbolises Christ—the 'fountain of life', who, in his Incarnation, is the man of sorrows weeping with tears of grief and pity for the blind sinfulness of man. (The 'her' in line 53 in no way invalidates this interpretation, since Vaughan commonly uses nouns with their Welsh gender.) Unfortunately this reading of the symbol is complicated by a difficult and possibly corrupt line—'And on the dumb shades language spent'. Without attempting any emendation, we may perhaps roughly paraphrase the line as follows: 'And, in addition to the message of the dumb shades, Christ himself expends on us the solace of his tears.' 'On' could be taken in the sense of 'over and above', 'in addition to'; and the 'shades' language' would refer to the beauty of religion, all the significance of the grove-garden, which is 'dumb' because it is addressed to the eye, not to the ear.

However, what matters in this poem is not so much Christ

---

[1] This is Vaughan's own wording as appended to *Religion*. If he is echoing this verse, he is drastically transforming the image, for besides being 'sealed', the fountain represents the Bride (the Church) not the Bridegroom (Christ).

[2] *Works*, p. 162, and *The Search* (ll. 22–32).

[3] See the interpolated lines 47–8 from the translation of Ovid's *De Ponto*, lib. 3, *The Search*, ll. 69–70; *Corruption*, ll. 23–8; 'They are all gone into the world of light', l. 23; *The Queer*, l. 8; *The Retirement* (*Thalia Rediviva*), l. 6.

himself as his symbolical significance as the fountain of life, which Vaughan elaborates to describe a further stage in the pilgrim's progress—his discovery of the spiritual condition of mankind in general and of the fact and mystery of predestination.

The symbolism and reference in Vaughan's first statement of this theme (ll. 53–60), though complex and a little strained in some respects, is easily accessible. The 'cistern' (probably not to be distinguished in any special way from the 'fountain' or the 'flood') is almost certainly a pointer to Jeremiah 2. 13, a reference that is singularly apt in one way but inappropriate in another: 'they have forsaken me the fountain of living waters, and hewed them out cisterns, broken cisterns, that can hold no water.' Stones as a symbolical representation of souls is not a common one, either generally or in Vaughan's writing; but the symbol has some Scriptural precedent[1] and is close to Vaughan's emblematic figure of the heart of 'flint' (even in the regenerate). The souls of the elect are 'bright' and 'round' because they are pure and perfect; while—possibly with some reminiscence of pebbles tossed and carried along by a vigorous mountain stream—Vaughan pictures them as dancing through the fountain of life, which is Christ, towards God and heaven. The souls of the unelect, in sharpest contrast, are 'ill-shap'd', 'dull', and 'nail'd to the centre', by which Vaughan means, as elsewhere in his writing,[2] earth and ultimately hell, located in the centre of the globe. This antithesis is intensified by two further details—the echo of the Scriptural 'first' and 'last', and the contrasting, highly characteristic similes of 'light' and 'night'. Fairly close parallels to this passage may be found in *Corruption*—

> Sin triumphs still, and man is sunk below
> The centre, and his shroud.
> All's in deep sleep and night

—and also in *Man in Darkness*: 'The flesh . . . draws us back to the Earth, as to its proper centre and original; but the soul being

[1] See Ezekiel 36. 26; Matthew 3. 9; and—though the reference is to living souls in the new Temple—1 Peter 2. 4–5.
[2] E.g. *Corruption*, l. 36. Herbert also uses 'centre' to mean earth and its interior (e.g. *The Search*, l. 7).

descended from the Father of Lights is like the sparks of fire still flying upwards.'[1]

Line 63, 'My restless eye, that still desir'd,' poses some small difficulty of interpretation. It may perhaps be taken as a simple narrative bridge, but the pointed description of the eye as restless and desiring seems to indicate some significant meaning. Probably Vaughan is referring to the poet-pilgrim's still unsatisfied quest for God, who has so far been experienced only in momentary revelations and who is not present in the first vision of the elect and unregenerate. The discovery of the 'ray' and the 'rushing wind' has yet to come; while even at the end of the pilgrimage the descent of the Holy Spirit can only be prayed for and awaited.

This small detail apart, the poem moves towards its close on a fairly simple and straightforward course. Stanza 9 commences with a second symbolical representation of the poet's belief in predestination. God is figured as the 'ray', and human souls are divided between those who stand open, 'broad-eyed', to the influence of the celestial light, and those who are 'fast asleep' (or in a state of spiritual torpor). This repetition of the theme of stanzas 7–8 is certainly compact and poetically effective; and the 'ray', the 'bank of flowers'—as well as the later 'leaves'—provide some satisfying recapitulation of earlier imagery. Perhaps, too, the restatement of theme adds something to the poem since the reference this time to the active ministration of God, reinforced by the phrase "twas mid-day', emphasises the hopeless blindness of those who remain 'nail'd to the centre'. On the other hand, as a whole the stanza cannot be completely defended against a charge of redundancy.

The final development in the poem is introduced by the 'rushing wind' that the pilgrim suddenly hears. This image, which brings the second of the two main hermetic representations of God[2] into one and the same poem, is undoubtedly an echo of

---

[1] *Works*, p. 315.
[2] It is also probable that Vaughan was intimating the third manifestation of the Trinity—God, Christ, and now the Holy Spirit.

Acts 2. 2: 'there came a sound from heaven as of a rushing mighty wind.' But much more significant in the concluding lines of the poem is the allusion, prompted most likely by the allegorical reading of *The Song of Songs* 4. 4, to one of the central New Testament texts on election and salvation, John 3. 3–8, and especially to verse 8: 'The wind bloweth where it listeth, and thou hearest the sound thereof, but canst not tell whence it cometh, and whither it goeth: so is everyone that is born of the spirit.' All through the last three stanzas the intellectual perplexity of the pilgrim, confronted with the mystery of election, is reiterated—'I wonder'd much', 'musing long', 'while I list'ning sought My mind to ease'; and Vaughan uses this text from John to point his conclusion. All musing and wondering is in vain, he intimates, for there is no rational human explanation of the mystery. The Christian can only submit to the inscrutable will and purpose of God, to the divine breath that whispers 'Where I please'. In exactly the same way he resolves the foiled questioning in his other important poem about election, *The World*; and the parallel between the two poems is particularly close since *The World* also contains the image of the Divine Sun:

> Yet some, who all this while did weep and sing,
> And sing, and weep, soar'd up into the ring;
>   But most would use no wing.
> O fools—said I—thus to prefer dark night
>   Before true light!
> To live in grots and caves, and hate the day
>   Because it shows the way;
> The way, which from this dead and dark abode
>   Leads up to God;
> A way where you might tread the sun, and be
>   More bright than he!
> But as I did their madness so discuss,
>   One whisper'd thus,
> 'This ring the Bridegroom did for none provide,
>   But for His bride.'

As it began, so the poem ends with a somewhat enigmatic line. 'And let me die before my death' cannot be Vaughan's con-

116

stant thought, plainly expressed in several other poems,[1] of the Christian's need to be continuously remembering his sojourn in the grave and so reconciling himself to death, for the 'one breath' (of divine grace) that he is invoking can have little to do with the discipline of mortification. Possibly he is alluding to the mystical 'mors raptus'[2] that Donne speaks of in one of his sermons: 'I will find out another death, mortem raptus, a death of rapture, of ecstasy, and that death which St Paul died more than once' (*LXXX Sermons*, No. 27). But from the total context of the poem, and its title, it seems much more likely that Vaughan is speaking here of the death of the old Adam in him that, in the dialectical process of Christian spiritual growth, must always precede the rebirth of the soul. We die in spirit to be reborn; and we can only be reborn after a spiritual death. As he writes in one of his translations from Paulinus:

> So blest in death and life, man dies to sins,
> And lives to God; sin dies, and life begins
> To be revived: old Adam falls away,
> And the new lives, born for eternal sway.[3]

Yet these lines, which concern baptism, do not provide a perfect gloss on the concluding couplet of *Regeneration*, for in *Regeneration* Vaughan is speaking of the spiritual death and rebirth that are dependent upon the 'one breath', upon predestination and the grace of God. Not completely sure of his election, in spite of abandonment of his old sinful ways and the revelations of God and Christian religion, the pilgrim-poet can only conclude with the humble prayer that the Holy Spirit will descend on him[4] and that he will be numbered among the elect.

---

[1] E.g., *Rules and Lessons*, ll. 125–6.

[2] Itrat-Husain (*The Mystical Element in the Metaphysical Poets of the Seventeenth Century*, p. 214) interprets the lines in this way as an intimation of that death of ecstasy that marks the final 'unitive' stage of mystical experience, the stage of oneness with the Absolute.

[3] *Works*, p. 365. See also *Ascension Hymn*, ll. 7–12, and the line in another translation from Paulinus—'I have died since, and have been born again' (p. 349, l.10).

[4] This would have been the accepted allegorical reading, sometimes indicated in the margin, of the text, *The Song of Songs* 4. 16, that Vaughan prints as his epigraph.

CHAPTER VII

'THE MORNING-WATCH'

O Joys! infinite sweetness! with what flowers
And shoots of glory, my soul breaks and buds!
  All the long hours
   Of night and rest,
   Through the still shrouds   5
   Of sleep, and clouds,
  This dew fell on my breast;
   O how it bloods,
And spirits all my earth! hark! in what rings,
And hymning circulations the quick world   10
   Awakes, and sings!
   The rising winds,
   And falling springs,
  Birds, beasts, all things
Adore Him in their kinds.   15
   Thus all is hurl'd
In sacred hymns and order; the great chime
And symphony of Nature. Prayer is
   The world in tune,
   A spirit-voice,   20
   And vocal joys,
  Whose echo is heaven's bliss.
   O let me climb
When I lie down! The pious soul by night
Is like a clouded star, whose beams, though said   25
   To shed their light
   Under some cloud,

Yet are above,
And shine and move
Beyond that misty shroud.   30
So in my bed,
That curtain'd grave, though sleep, like ashes, hide
My lamp and life, both shall in Thee abide.

THERE is probably no better way of initiating oneself into Vaughan's poetry than through *The Morning-Watch*, for besides being certainly one of his two or three finest lyrics it is perhaps the most abundantly characteristic.

The word 'Watch', in the title, points clearly to the poem's essentially devotional nature, its central inspiration in certain religious ideas, sentiments, and experiences that were for Vaughan always associated with night and daybreak; and there are several passages in his book of 'Solitary Devotions', *The Mount of Olives*, that approach the poem very closely. For a devotion that parallels the lyric in its sentiments and spiritual inclination there is, for instance, the morning prayer that reads:

O Thou! that never slumberest nor sleepest, how careful hast Thou been of me! how hast Thou protected me, and with Thy holy angels, Thy ministering spirits sent forth to minister for the heirs of salvation, encompassed me about! Yea, with what immeasureable love hast Thou restored unto me the light of day, and raised me from sleep and the shadow of death to look up to Thy holy hill. Justly mightst Thou, O God, have shut the gates of death upon me, and laid me for ever under the bars of the earth, but Thou hast redeemed me from corruption, and with Thy everlasting arms enlarged my time of repentance.[1]

Another passage in *The Mount of Olives* that provides a most interesting parallel with the poem in its pattern of references to hymns, order, stars, beds, sleep, the dew that falls by night, is the opening meditation:

[1] *Works*, p. 145.

I   119   F.P.L.

The night, saith Chrysostom, was not therefore made that either we should sleep it out, or pass it away idly; and chiefly because we see many worldly persons to watch out whole nights for the commodities of this life. In the primitive Church also the Saints of God used to rise at midnight to praise the Rock of their salvation with hymns and spiritual songs. In the same manner shouldst thou do now, and contemplate the order of the stars, and how they all in their several stations praise their Creator. When all the world is asleep, thou shouldst watch, weep and pray and propose unto thyself that practice of the Psalmist, *I am weary of my groaning, every night wash I my bed, and water my couch with my tears*; for as the dew which falls by night is most fructifying, and tempers the heat of the sun, so the tears we shed in the night make the soul fruitful, quench all concupiscence, and supple the hardness we got in the day.[1]

Whether or not we share these profound devotional experiences out of which the poem certainly springs, there can be no doubt that the two opening lines, charged with an intense exhilaration and excitement, at once communicate a most rich and joyous affirmation of life. That is their widest reference. More particularly, they express a sense of that elemental, surprised delight and gratitude that most of us, believers or not, feel at our waking return to consciousness and life; a sense, too, through such words as 'flowers', 'shoots', 'buds', of freshness, renewal, re-creation—and apprehension that Vaughan elsewhere crystallises in the line,

> But mornings new creations are.[2]
>
> *The Day Spring*

Again, responding to these opening lines in another way, we shall not be distorting the poem if we allow 'joys' and 'sweetness' to evoke images of the earth's revived beauty at daybreak, in particular of the stirring breezes and the sounds of birds and water that are mentioned later in the poem. On the other hand, if we wish to keep close to Vaughan's experience, we should

[1] *Works*, p. 143.

[2] Cf. Elizabeth Holmes, *Henry Vaughan and the Hermetic Philosophy*, p. 17: 'Vaughan could experience an ordinary awakening from sleep as a kind of rebirth . . . and feel that in sleep some process of purification, of re-integration at a primal source, had been at work upon him.'

120

notice that there is remarkably little description of sensuous beauty in the poem and that in the two opening lines, for all the nearly overwhelming surface impact of the metaphor, the main stress is on 'soul'. Above all else, the joys and sweetness that Vaughan feels, the primary impulse behind his rich vegetal image of Spring-time and revival, stem from the renewed assurance of his soul's immortality. For him night and death were always terribly and profoundly synonymous; hence the significant, twice repeated reference to the 'shrouds' of sleep. Once again, under God's cherishing mercy, he has been literally resurrected; and as we read the opening we feel in it the triumphant vindication of the faith that is expressed in the close, for the lyric turns in a perfect circle of development:

> So in my bed,
> That curtain'd grave, though sleep, like ashes, hide
> My lamp and life, both shall in Thee abide.

There is still more to the compacted richness of the opening. The sense of 'glory' that Vaughan so exultantly communicates is not limited to the realisation that his soul is a divine spark, resurrected, immortal, and cherished by God. God's glory is also manifest in his Creation and in his morning revival of it, and through the perfect vegetal metaphor of his soul's awakening Vaughan expresses—unusual though this is in his poetry—a conviction of inseparable fusion with this Creation, so that a few lines later he can speak of 'my earth'. His soul is both a shoot of glory itself and at the same time absorbed in a wider glory.

The passage that follows down to lines 9 and 10, turning chiefly on the 'dew' image,[1] serves mainly to amplify the first two lines. In its reference to the poet 'dew' is of course to be taken primarily in its symbolical sense of divine grace and spirit,

[1] It is interesting to note that the passage quoted on p. 119 from the morning prayer, 'O Thou! that never slumberest', etc., is shortly followed by the supplication, 'supple my heart with the dew of Thy divine Spirit' (*Works*, p. 145). Henry Vaughan may have been familiar with his brother's notion of dew as both a material and spiritual substance. According to Thomas Vaughan dew contained star-fire and therefore ultimately the Divine Radiance: 'dew hath in it some small dose of the star-fire' (*Euphrates*, *Works*, ed. by A. E. Waite, p. 425).

though if anything of the literal meaning does obtrude into the line, 'This dew fell on my breast', there is nothing grotesque in the image, thanks to the impression left by the opening lines. For God, on the other hand, the two meanings of the word apply equally : with the dew as physical substance he has virtually nurtured the world—hence 'bloods ... my earth';[1] at the same time, after the deathly sleep of night, he has renewed or restored his spirit, which for Vaughan was always present 'in all things, though invisibly'. So the phrase 'my earth' signifies not only the poet's absorption in Nature but a community with the divine spirit.

Apart from these implications of the dew image and the special significance of 'shrouds', this part of the poem is relatively straightforward. But it gathers some complexity as it modulates into the next section. These lines certainly carry a definite reference to that water–blood–spirit complex that has been examined earlier,[2] and probably, through 'blood', 'rings', 'circulation', and 'quick', an allusion to Harvey's discovery of the circulation of the blood. Further, though this is much more dubious, Mrs Joan Bennett[3] may be right in reading in lines 8–9 a reference to the older physiological theory that the vital spirits were created by the blood in the heart.

These complex bridge-lines both momentarily sustain the opening theme of life's renewal (notably in the words 'the quick world Awakes') and at the same time, with 'hymning circulations' and again with 'sings', introduce the next—that of Nature, inanimate as well as animate, ever intent on its Creator and ever, to the shame of neglectful man, worshipping and adoring him. But this most familiar conception of Vaughan's here takes a rather specialised form, for it is the music of the earth ('the

---

[1] There may well be a deliberate ambiguity here, 'earth' also signifying the physical body. Such an ambiguity could effectively link the earlier ' breast' with 'quick world'. In any event the general meaning of these lines is certainly that the Divine dew penetrates and transforms all that is physical—the poet's body and the morning world.

[2] See pp. 42–7.

[3] *Four Metaphysical Poets*, second ed., p. 84, Note 1.

singing of birds is *naturalis musica mundi*, to which all arted strains are but discord and hardness')[1] that he stresses; and the introductory 'hymning circulations' rises to the magnificent climax of 'the great chime And symphony of Nature'. On the other hand, it is probably a distortion of Vaughan's meaning to associate the idea of music too completely with sound, for he has several passages—the *naturalis musica mundi* one just quoted, for instance—that suggest he had little fondness for music;[2] and we cannot ignore that bare, philosophical word 'order' that obtrudes between 'sacred hymns' and 'the great chime And symphony of Nature'. For these reasons it is probable that what he chiefly had in mind was the old mediaeval idea, moribund in general but revived for him by his hermetic reading, of the divinely ordained hierarchy of Nature, and that we should take 'chime' and 'symphony' mainly in the generalised sense of 'concord', 'harmony', etc., and so in line with 'order' as essentially philosophical terms.

The next passage ('Prayer is The World in tune,' etc.) is both a brief recapitulation—perhaps a little too repetitive—and a preparation for the close of the poem. 'World in tune', the most obvious and immediate link, 'spirit-voice' (because Nature is infused with the divine spirit), and 'vocal joys' are all summary phrases of what has gone before; but, articulated in a rather flat, prose-like statement, they also serve to formulate a definition of prayer, which is an alternative way of regarding the sounds and motion of Nature.

Reminded of this spiritual resource of prayer, and fortified by it, Vaughan's meditation turns back again to the day's antithesis —'climb' in his apostrophe (or colloquy) meaning 'pray'.[3] Thus the concluding section of the poem consists of a restatement, in

[1] *Works*, p. 177.
[2] Cf. E. W. Williamson, *Henry Vaughan*, p. 18: 'It seems improbable that Vaughan shared the Welshman's delight in music; and certainly, as practised in human society, he disapproved its *coarse measures, false juggling sounds*, which made grave music *like wild wit*.' For special reference to *The Morning-Watch* see Williamson's Note 15: 'The *chime and symphony* of Nature probably goes beyond natural sounds, but it includes them.'
[3] For 'climb' as prayer see, for example, *Isaac's Marriage*, ll. 44-5.

more emphatic terms, of the second. On the one hand, with the phrases 'misty shroud' and 'curtain'd grave'—and possibly the punning use of 'ashes'[1]—he stresses more strongly than before the death associations of sleep and night. On the other, he now conceives of the night as a time of active and to some extent voluntary spiritual life: the soul is no longer imaged as a dew-washed plant but as a beaming star, 'clouded' by sleep and the physical body but never eclipsed. The 'beams' of the star-soul that 'shine and move' almost certainly signify those rare, God-tending thoughts and intuitions that he believed to be a special blessing of the perilous night hours, while implied in the whole passage there is probably a conception of night as a time of particularly close communion with God[2]—a conception that is the core of another great poem, *The Night*. Be that as it may, the lyric ends unmistakably on a characteristic note of serene assurance in God.

One detail in the concluding couplet, the word 'lamp', presents some difficulty of interpretation. No doubt of course that in a general sort of way the metaphor stands for the soul, as it does in *The Relapse* (ll. 13–16) and 'Silence, and stealth of days' (l. 7 ff.). Yet in view of the ideas in lines 24–30 'lamp' cannot signify the entire soul, part of which is above earth and still beaming. Possibly by 'lamp' Vaughan means the rational part of the soul that deliberately searches for God, whereas the 'pious soul' is the divine spark or star-fire in man sympathetically attracted to its origin in God. There are some lines in *The Feast* (43–8) which, though their reference is to God, would support this interpretation of 'lamp'.

[1] In *Rules and Lessons*, ll. 128–34, the reference to night-time prayer is also followed by an image of ash-smothered fire.

[2] See *Man in Darkness, Works*, p. 169: 'It is an observation of some spirits, that *the night is the mother of thoughts*. And I shall add that those thoughts are stars, the scintillations and lightnings of the soul struggling with darkness. This antipathy in her is radical, for being descended from the *house of light*, she hates a contrary principle and being at that time a prisoner in some measure to an enemy, she becomes pensive, and full of thoughts.'

See also *The Mount of Olives*, p. 152: 'Enlighten my soul, sanctify my body, govern my affections, and guide my thoughts, that in the fastest closures of my eyelids my spirit may see Thee, and in depth of sleep be conversant with Thee.'

Short as the lyric is, it is by no means flawless. Its chief weakness is a loss of tension in the lines on prayer (18–22). The general tone of this passage is flat, and there is some repetition both in ideas and in the nature of the rhythmical phrasing. Again, the second night-description (ll. 24–31) is marred by the redundancy of 'clouded star' and 'Under some cloud', and also—especially for those who know Vaughan's work well—by the much overworked *cloud-shroud* rhyme, already employed before in the poem. For a smaller blemish there is the rhyme-forced, inappropriate use of 'hurl'd' (correctly employed for its connotation of violent agitation, disorder, etc., in *Distraction*, l. 12, and *The World*, l. 7) in a context of 'sacred hymns and order'.

So far as sound texture is concerned the prominent alliteration usually pleases and sometimes concentrates attention, while now and then there are some satisfying, more delicate internal alliterations—as of the *l* consonant in

> All the long hours
> Of night and rest,
> Through the still shrouds
> Of sleep, and clouds. . . .

On the other hand, there is very little chiming and patterning of recurrent vowels, nor does the sound ever serve, in any notable way, to suggest or reinforce meaning or sense-impression. The rhythm, too, lacks any subtlety or particularly suggestive effect.

However, these defects and limitations count for little beside the great and unmistakable achievements of the poem. High among these must be set its admirable, arresting opening: admirable, especially, for its bold metaphor which compacts so much meaning and significance, and for the phrase 'shoots of glory', which, though it is almost certainly lifted from Felltham,[1] is stamped with Vaughan's own individual sensibility and, like 'chime And symphony of Nature', possesses that peculiar felicity that one finds so often in Shakespeare, the Authorized

[1] Felltham's *Resolves*, 'Of the Soul'—'The conscience, the character of a God stampt in it, and the apprehension of Eternity, do all prove it a shoot of everlastingness.'

Version of the Bible, and early seventeenth-century writing generally—an immediate conjunction of the concrete and abstract that, engaging senses and intellect together, instantaneously irradiates the material and brings the abstract and ideal down to earth. 'Sweetness'—another echo probably from Herbert's poetry, where the word is recurrent—is also a most happy touch, since it is one of the few emotive terms of delight that are still comparatively undebased.

With this compulsive, most lyrical opening goes a memorable and satisfying close, which, besides returning us to the beginning, admirably balances with it—in the two long, five-stress lines (appropriately varied by a conclusive rhyme), in the similar density of metaphor, and, above all, in the fact that it epitomises Vaughan's night sensations, the terror and the assurance, as the opening epitomises his spiritual exhilaration at daybreak.

For another pleasing structural correspondence we may observe how the opening is followed, and the close preceded, by a description, in shorter lines, of night. Without being unduly repetitive, the second passage recalls the first by its reference to 'cloud' and 'shroud', though at the cost of a repeated rhyme; while the two sections also match in that each is dominated by a single spiritual metaphor, 'dew' in one instance and 'star' in the other. Between these two passages there is a vision of the awakened earth at daybreak in which all the harmonious activities of Nature are represented first as hymns and then, in a conception that carries us right through to the end of the poem, as prayer.

In sum, the lyric is most firmly organised, with wholeness, balance, and continuity.

On paper it may appear rather formal in its patterning of long and short lines (which Professor Kermode has condemned as 'brusquely opposed'),[1] and its rhyme scheme is a fairly complicated one. Yet it reads well, and never sounds in any way constrained, over-ingenious, or mechanically contrived. Part of

[1] 'The Private Imagery of Henry Vaughan', *R.E.S.*, New Series, vol. I, no. 3, p. 208.

Vaughan's success lies in his resourceful variations of phrase and cadence. One has only to compare the diverse rhythms of the pairs of long lines to appreciate this. Again, there is much skilful, and satisfying, enjambement between the long and short lines. But chiefly he avoids the worst kind of metrical artificiality because the rhymes and shortened lines are never in control, as they might so easily be; they are crossed with, and subordinate to, fluent speech rhythms and constructions. This rhythmical achievement is particularly noticeable in the sections of shortened lines, where the dangerously brief phrases and the close proximity of rhyming words rarely impede the sustained flow of the poem:

> The pious soul by night
> Is like a clouded star, whose beams, though said
> To shed their light
> Under some cloud,
> Yet are above,
> And shine and move
> Beyond that misty shroud.

The language represents Vaughan at his best—a triumph in the direct, concrete, simple, usually monosyllabic kind of diction, with nothing wasted—

> . . . my soul breaks and buds.

> This dew fell on my breast.

> O let me climb
> When I lie down.

'Bloods . . . my earth' is a good example of Vaughan's occasional and generally felicitous use of a concrete noun as a verb. And, for a pleasing variety, there is now and then a touch of the abstract and polysyllabic, like 'hymning circulations'.

Finally, among the achievements of this poem, there is its compacted richness of meaning and imaginative effect—a quality indicated (but not too prosaically laboured, one hopes) in the first section of this chapter.

In spite of its outstanding excellence and originality, *The Morning-Watch* is exceptionally indebted to Herbert (none of Vaughan's major lyrics more so), and though Herbert's influence has already been generally considered, it should be of some interest to look again at this subject in the concentrated context of a particular poem.

The first echo occurs in the opening words, which were obviously prompted by the beginning of Herbert's *The Holy Scriptures*—'O Book! infinite sweetness.' Vaughan's repetition of 'infinite sweetness', as well as his apostrophic construction, may have been an unconscious recollection, but it seems much more likely that we have an instance here of deliberate exploitation and adaptation of a borrowing : he is using the Herbert phrase—and probably its context—for the implied assertion that the 'Book of Nature' is truly comparable with the Book of the Scriptures for the divine lessons that it contains.

There are two other instances of what are most probably intended as pointed quotations from Herbert. Lines 10–15 ('the quick world Awakes, and sings,' etc.)—themselves very close to lines 7–12 in *Christ's Nativity*—clearly derive from a stanza in Herbert's *Providence* :

> Man is the world's High Priest : he doth present
> The sacrifice for all; while they below
> Unto the service mutter an assent
> Such as springs use that fall, and winds that blow.

Bearing in mind the prominence in Vaughan's poetry of this idea of a worshipful Creation, his several repetitions of the 'wind'–'spring' conjunction, and his reference in *Christ's Nativity* to man as the 'high priest' of Nature, we can be fairly certain that these lines from *Providence* were vividly imprinted in his mind. If this recollection was a conscious one, it would appear that he has pointed it by his exclusion of man from the Creation's hymn of praise. It is also interesting to note that he has for once preserved the context of his borrowing.

The second example of a seemingly deliberate quotation is the two lines, 'Thus all is hurl'd In sacred hymns and order', which (perhaps accounting for the inappropriate use of 'hurl'd') echo a line from *Doomsday*, 'Man is out of order hurl'd' (l. 27). Here Vaughan is probably using his quotation, with a significant twist, to underline the contrast between the order of Nature and the disorder of man. This contrast is one of his central ideas, and it would fit in with the exclusion of 'Man is the world's High Priest' from the previous quotation.

(In passing, we may notice that the context of the *Doomsday* line carries a reference to music—

> Lord, thy broken consort raise,
> And the music shall be praise

—which may have had a subconscious influence on Vaughan's 'chime' and 'symphony' and something of what follows.)

Another obvious link with Herbert's poetry is to be found in the lines,

> Prayer is
> The world in tune,
> A spirit-voice,
> And vocal joys
> Whose echo is heaven's bliss.

These lines derive largely from two passages in *Prayer I* :

[1]

A kind of tune, which all things hear and fear. . . .

[2]

Softness, and peace, and joy, and love, and bliss. . . .
Heaven in ordinary.

Here it is likely that both recollections (and certainly the second, which is simply one of isolated, scattered words) were purely subconscious. In a similar sort of way it is possible that yet another line from *Prayer I*—

Church bells beyond the stars heard, the soul's blood . . .

—may have inspired Vaughan's 'chime' and the lines,

> O how it bloods,
> And spirits all my earth!

Added together, these quotations from Herbert amount to a considerable sum of indebtedness. On the other hand, it would be wrong to say, as Professor Kermode does in his essay on Vaughan, that the predominant inspiration in *The Morning-Watch* is a literary one. A sympathetic assimilation of all Vaughan's writing can leave the reader in little doubt that this lyric springs directly and primarily, not from his admittedly retentive reading of Herbert, but from his own devotional life and from the central and individual world of his own imaginative experience—from his deep sensibility to night and daybreak and the complex of religious ideas and sentiments peculiarly associated with these times. There are numerous passages in his other poems and in *The Mount of Olives* that bring us infinitely closer to *The Morning-Watch* than anything in *The Temple* ever does.

Space will not allow a detailed consideration of Kermode's argument, which both ignores Vaughan's active and purposeful manipulation of several of his borrowings and greatly exaggerates their inspirational effect. Two examples of this exaggeration must suffice. The first is his assertion that there is a rhythmic parallel (as well as an echo of phrase) between Vaughan's opening lines and Herbert's

> O Book! infinite sweetness, let my heart
> Suck every letter, and a honey gain.
>
> *The Holy Scriptures I*

Here one can only conclude that Kermode's usually sensitive ear went deaf on him, for in speed, texture, and rhythmic phrasing these two passages are as distinct as could possibly be.

A second example of over-stress is his contention that Herbert's *Prayer I* exercises a 'germinal' inspiration, first, because the line, 'A kind of tune, which all things hear and fear,' along with 'Church bells beyond the stars heard, the soul's blood,' serves as Vaughan's 'initial impulse to use the musical metaphor' in lines 9–18, and secondly, because it produces the transition from prayer to music.

There may, just possibly, be something in the first point, though from the evidence of many other poems of Vaughan one can argue that this idea of the *naturalis musica mundi* was too familiar and deeply ingrained in his imagination to require any impulse from Herbert for its poetic expression. But so far as the development of the poem is concerned, hymns and prayers are so close for Vaughan, almost synonymous, in this context of man and the Creation praising God at daybreak that it is quite unnecessary to suggest any submerged or outside determinant. It is much more reasonable to think of him making his own modulation of theme, without any prompting from Herbert, though perhaps subconsciously recalling his phrase about prayer, 'A kind of tune', and admitting it as a convenient link in his own poem.

At the beginning of this chapter reference was made to the exceptionally representative quality of *The Morning-Watch*. It is a poem that memorably expresses something at the heart of Vaughan's imaginative experience, his intense, complex, and continuous awareness of the alternation of day and night.[1] Hence, as we read it, we are constantly reminded of this or that passage in his other poems, for instance of such lines as

> When first thy eyes unveil, give thy soul leave
> To do the like; our bodies but forerun
> The spirit's duty. True hearts spread and heave
> Unto their God, as flow'rs do to the sun.
> Give Him thy first thoughts then; so shalt thou keep
> Him company all day, and in Him sleep. . . .

> Walk with thy fellow-creatures : note the hush
> And whispers among them. There's not a spring
> Or leaf but hath his morning-hymn. Each bush
> And oak doth know I AM. Canst thou not sing?
> O leave thy cares and follies! go this way,
> And thou art sure to prosper all the day. . . .

[1] See pp. 9–10.

> Mornings are mysteries; the first world's youth,
> Man's resurrection, and the Future's bud
> Shroud in their births. . . .[1]

More particularly, the highly characteristic quality of *The Morning-Watch* arises from the fact that almost all of its main images are widely recurrent, often as key symbols, in Vaughan's poetry as a whole.

For instance, the opening is but one of innumerable examples of his fondness for vegetal metaphors to describe his spiritual state. As in these lines, he frequently expresses feelings of spiritual revival, recovery, exceptional responsiveness—and sometimes of hope and expectation—through images of buds, shoots, leaves and flowers, these often under the cherishing influence of dew, showers, light, or warm sunshine. Another most memorable example of this kind of image (much indebted also to Felltham) is the one in *The Retreat*:

> But felt through all this fleshly dress
> Bright shoots of everlastingness.

When, on the other hand, he wishes to convey a sense of spiritual affliction and defeat he commonly represents the plant- or flower-soul as blasted by frosts or winds, though sometimes, as in *Love and Discipline* (1. 11) and *Affliction* ll. 11–16), frost is regarded as a beneficial rather than a deadly force, destroying the weeds and thistles of the soul.

It is a measure of the importance of this image that it furnishes much of the substance of three entire poems, *Unprofitableness*, *Love and Discipline*, and *The Sap*; and the first of these, by far the best of the three lyrics, is particularly interesting for its combination of the image of the storm-blasted and dew-revived plant.

References to dew are to be found everywhere; and it was a most happy inspiration that led Sassoon, in his fine poem on Vaughan, to describe him as one

---

[1] See also *Christ's Nativity*, ll. 9–12, *The Bird*, ll. 7–18, *Providence*, ll. 22–30, *The Dawning*, ll. 9–21, *The Day of Judgment*, ll. 1–14, and—from *Thalia Rediviva* —*The Revival*, ll. 1–8, *The Day Spring*, ll. 13–16, *The Bee*, ll. 35–46.

whose name flows on for ever
Through pastures of the spirit washed with dew.[1]

As Vaughan had first used the image in two of his early secular poems it had been merely the conventional cliché for lovers' tears, but in *Silex Scintillans* he magically and richly transformed it, both intensifying its literal and sensuous impression and at the same time employing it as one of his key, co-ordinating symbols for tears of repentance (or pity) and for the ministration of divine grace, especially of a healing, reviving, or saving kind. Out of this transformation came some of his loveliest lines like

> A grief, whose silent dew shall breed
> Lilies and myrrh.
>
> *Jesus Weeping II*

Water, including of course dew, constitutes one of his richest, most widespread symbols and images;[2] and the 'falling springs' of *The Morning-Watch* reminds us of the countless references in his poetry to springs, wells, fountains, waterfalls, streams and rivers, as well as to rain and showers. Much of the inspiration here was no doubt derived from the Bible, whether from its landscape or from the symbolical significance of verses like *The Song of Songs* 4. 12 and 15 or 1 John 5. 6–8. But equally important must have been the daily impression of his own countryside and his sensuous delight in the sound and movement of water, a pleasure that we can trace in his earliest poems, in lines like

> And crystal springs shall drop thee melody,
>
> *In Amicum Foeneratorem*

and

> Like to the wat'ry music of some spring.
>
> *To Sir William D'avenant*[3]

Symbolism and Scriptural precedent apart, we can be fairly certain that he would have applauded Samuel Palmer's sentiment,

---

[1] *At the Grave of Henry Vaughan.*   [2] See p. 43

[3] See also the long descriptive passage of the 'crystal spring' in *Monsieur Gombauld*, ll. 31–40.

'Never forget the charm of running water';[1] and even in *Silex Scintillans*, amid so much occult water-symbolism, whether Biblical or hermetic, there are moments when we surely catch the delight of pure, native sensibility, as when, in his picture of the newly-created world, he tells us how

> Springs, like dissolved pearls, their streams did pour
> Ne'er marr'd with floods.

Ascension Day

Again, it is entirely typical of him that in a poem of imaginings about Christ's earthly place of meditation (*The Dwelling-Place*) he strikes out as his first line

> What happy, secret fountain. . . .

Miss Mahood has already pointed out much of the significance of this water-imagery.[2] But stressing its importance in a group of 'fructification images'—as, for instance, in the form of 'living waters' (Christ, eternal life)—she has both oversimplified its wide symbolical significance and ignored the very diverse illustrative purposes that it serves. At one time Vaughan will find in a waterfall a solacing emblem of resurrection; at another, in *The Dawning* (ll. 33–6, etc.) he envies a spring for it freshness and motion.[3] On the other hand, the waterfall of *Misery* (ll. 9–16) represents the blind abandon of thoughts that draw him towards spiritual destruction, while the stream in *The Mutiny* is evoked for its foam and 'frothy noise' and its similarity to the turmoil of his own rebellious soul. For a further measure of his variety there is that strange well at the beginning of *Abel's blood*, which is probably a fusion of Genesis 4. 10 with recollection of a Llansantffraed spring that sometimes, like the river Usk,[4] ran a reddish colour.

[1] Quoted in the *Biographical Introduction* to the Victoria and Albert Museum Catalogue of an exhibition of Palmer's work in 1926.

[2] *Poetry and Humanism*, p. 278.

[3] An occasional antithetical image to the flowing stream is the puddle, an emblem for spiritual stagnation, etc. See *Religion*, l. 43, *The Dawning*, ll. 29–33, and *Daphnis*, ll. 149–50.

[4] Hutchinson, *op. cit.*, pp. 21–2.

Wind constitutes another important item in Vaughan's imagery, though it is much less prominent, and complex in treatment, than his frequent references to water. 'The rising winds'
of *The Morning-Watch* are literally conceived (apart, that is,
from their contribution to the morning-hymn of the Creation);
but more often wind is a symbol of the Divine breath, as in the
lines,

> There's not a wind can stir,
> Or beam pass by,
> But straight I think, though far,
> Thy hand is nigh.
> > 'Come, come! What do I here'

This particular symbolisation of wind was no doubt indeterminately derived from both hermetic and Biblical reading; and
one of Vaughan's obvious Scriptural inspirations (*The Song of
Songs* 4. 16) probably accounts for the fact that in several poems
wind is associated with those countryside scents of which he
seems to have been particularly fond.[1] On the other hand, wind
does not always signify divine influence; nor is it invariably
douce and beneficial. With frost, it sometimes represents the
forces of destruction, the 'snarling blasts', shattering the leaves
and flowers of his soul—

> And surly winds
> Blasted my infant buds.
> > *Regeneration*

(This conjunction of winds and springs in *The Morning-
Watch*, deriving almost certainly from a line in Herbert's
Providence, is also to be found in *Christ's Nativity* l. 8, *The Bird*
l. 15, and *The Bee* l. 29.)

With 'clouded star'[2] we come to another of the three or four
master images and symbols of Vaughan's poetry, 'star' standing
for God, the spiritual guidance of the saints and the illustrious
dead, and sometimes (as in *The Morning-Watch*) for the human
soul, and 'clouded' for some obstruction or 'veil' to the working of

---

[1] See, for example, *Mount of Olives II*, ll. 3–6.
[2] See pp. 24–6 for an analysis of this compound image in its subconscious forms.

these good influences—the physical body, sleep, sin, the world's corruption. Fundamentally, of course, this image must always signify the deprivation and frustration of fallen man and of mortal life. Nevertheless, Vaughan invests it with a considerable variety of tone. Sometimes, as we should naturally expect, grief is predominant:

> we shall there no more
> Watch stars, or pore
> Through melancholy clouds, and say,
>   'Would it were Day!'
>
> *Resurrection and Immortality*

But at other times there is gratitude, even joy, for what is received in spite of the frustration—as in *The Morning-Watch*, or in these lines from *White Sunday*:

> And yet, as in Night's gloomy page
> One silent star may interline;
> So in this last and lewdest age
> Thy ancient love on some may shine;

and it is truly indicative of Vaughan's serene, unrebellious nature that this essential image of deprivation is more often toned to gratitude than to repining wretchedness. Indeed, there are moments when he suggests that the stars, and all they symbolise, are the more beautiful and impressive for their eclipsing clouds:

>   and so the light
> When put out gains a value from the night.
> How glad are we, when but one twinkling star
> Peeps betwixt clouds more black than is our tar.
>
> *Daphnis*

Finally, as we have already seen, the lines 'my bed That curtain'd grave', are one example of a marked and interesting image-cluster in Vaughan's poetry. Also, constituent details apart, the image is infused with some of his deepest and most characteristic sentiments—sentiments that are echoed and epitomised, with a richly meaningful pun, by a modern writer who had probably read him with attention :

He wouldn't wish any thought, however long and pleasing, to remind him that bed-time was come : 'bed-time' that, in the way of symbolism, might be called 'grave-time' too.

T. F. Powys, Mr Weston's Good Wine

CHAPTER VIII

'THE NIGHT'

Through that pure virgin shrine,
That sacred veil drawn o'er Thy glorious noon,
That men might look and live, as glow-worms shine,
    And face the moon:
    Wise Nicodemus saw such light
    As made him know his God by night.

    Most blest believer he!
Who in that land of darkness and blind eyes
Thy long-expected healing wings could see
    When Thou didst rise!   10
    And, what can never more be done,
    Did at midnight speak with the Sun!

    O who will tell me, where
He found Thee at that dead and silent hour?
What hallow'd solitary ground did bear   15
    So rare a flower;
    Within whose sacred leaves did lie
    The fulness of the Deity?

    No mercy-seat of gold,
No dead and dusty cherub, nor carv'd stone,   20
But His own living works did my Lord hold
    And lodge alone;
    Where trees and herbs did watch and peep
    And wonder, while the Jews did sleep.

    Dear Night! this world's defeat;   25
The stop to busy fools; care's check and curb;
The day of spirits; my soul's calm retreat
    Which none disturb!
  Christ's progress, and His prayer-time;
  The hours to which high Heaven doth chime.   30

    God's silent, searching flight;
When my Lord's head is fill'd with dew, and all
His locks are wet with the clear drops of night;
    His still, soft call;
  His knocking-time; the soul's dumb watch,   35
  When spirits their fair kindred catch.

    Were all my loud, evil days
Calm and unhaunted as is thy dark tent,
Whose peace but by some angel's wing or voice
    Is seldom rent;   40
  Then I in heaven all the long year
  Would keep, and never wander here.

    But living where the sun
Doth all things wake, and where all mix and tire
Themselves and others, I consent and run   45
    To ev'ry mire:
  And by this world's ill-guiding light,
  Err more than I can do by night.

    There is in God—some say—
A deep, but dazzling darkness; as men here   50
Say it is late and dusky, because they
    See not all clear.
  O for that Night! where I in Him
  Might live invisible and dim!

THE obvious complement of *The Morning-Watch*, in imaginative orientation and spiritual experience, is *The Night*, another of Vaughan's masterpieces and perhaps his greatest poem.

Instantly in motion, with an inevitable, assured movement, from its opening line, and still moving powerfully till the firm finality of its close, the lyric is singularly wave-like in its broad rhythmical impact—four distinct waves that, with one exception, all roll back on themselves to some extent. The third wave, consisting of stanzas 5 and 6, is the deepest, most resounding and majestic—and the most magical in effect; but this does not produce anti-climax, for the fourth wave, sustained through three stanzas instead of two, is also highly impressive.

There is a similar wave-like effect in the internal movement of the stanzas, which are almost miniatures of the poem as a whole—the mounting from a three- to a five-stress line, the holding of this weight (usually with the slightest of pauses, or none at all, at the end of the second line) through two lines; the sudden fall to a two-stress line; and the momentary recovery, the fringe and surge, of the last two, four-stress lines, which, as rhymed couplets, terminate the stanzas with finality and emphasis. Within this common stanza pattern Vaughan achieves an outstanding rhythmical variety that is immensely pleasing, and, for an example of extremes, the reader might compare the cadences and placings of pause in stanza 5 with those in stanza 8.

This wave-like motion and fluidity is combined with a notable weightiness, which is chiefly produced by terminating lines with two speaking stresses, or something very close to that degree of accentuation—

> Who in that land of darkness and blind eyes,

and

> No dead and dusty cherub, nor carv'd stone.

There are some eight or nine examples of this weighted deceleration at the end of lines—a high proportion. The same spondaic effect is quite common internally, and stanza 5, by far the most slow moving in the poem, is outstanding in this respect:

Dear Night! this world's defeat;
The stop to busy fools; care's check and curb;
The day of spirits; my soul's calm retreat
        Which none disturb!
Christ's progress, and His pray(er)-time;
The hours to which high Heaven doth chime.

In its melodic texture most of the poem, like the rest of
Vaughan's work, is fairly plain spun. As usual there is a good
deal of alliteration, but with one or two exceptions—the internal
r's in the first two lines, for instance, which produce a softening,
slightly blurring sound effect, very appropriate to the context—
this alliteration is merely pleasant or emphatic, never contribut-
ing much to the meaning and enactment of the poem. However,
there is one stanza of rare and unmistakable aural beauty. This is
the sixth, where, though much is borrowed, Vaughan has combined a rich and highly suggestive melodic pattern with some
vivid and arresting imagery to give us one of his most glorious
passages. Particularly satisfying among the strands of this sound
pattern are the penetrating long *i*'s and closely alliterated *s*'s in
the first line—

God's silent, searching flight

—which suggests a shooting-star's rapidity of motion; the continuous liquidity of the *l* alliteration and the less obtrusive play
with the *d* consonant; and, above all, the repeated *o* vowel of
'God', 'locks', 'drops', 'soft', 'knocking'—a soft, ghostly, but
insistent sound that admirably conveys the manner of the divine
visitation.

In its subject the poem is one that is to some extent inspired
by a Biblical text (John 3. 2), and the first four stanzas read
unmistakably as a deliberate poetic meditation on the phrase,
'came to Jesus by night'. Vaughan's first variation on the phrase
is a picture of Nicodemus recognising the God in Christ by the
radiance that streams from him; and he elaborates and particu-
larises this picture through one of his favourite images—that of

the veil of the physical body over the luminous soul. But the 'shrine' and 'sacred veil' of Christ's human form is not the frustrating, corruptible body that he so often laments elsewhere in his poetry : it is Virgin-born and immaculate (both of these ideas are happily compressed in the ambiguity of the first line); it dims but does not eclipse the divine light within.

This image also enables Vaughan to enrich his first stanza with a wider reference—a joyous intimation of the consequences for all men of the Incarnation. Behind his phrase 'sacred veil' we may catch an echo of that verse from the Epistle to the Hebrews that he attaches to his poem *Resurrection and Immortality* : 'By a new and living way, which he hath consecrated for us, through the veil, that is to say, his flesh' (10. 20).[1] Through the 'veil', or Incarnation, a new way of spiritual life is open to men, a direct knowledge of God never possible before, a hallowing of the flesh and an assurance of resurrection. And even if we miss (or reject) this echo, there is little mistaking Vaughan's explicit restatement of the 'new and living way', namely the line, 'That men might look and live.'

Unfortunately this affirmation is ravelled up in the somewhat baffling glow-worm simile of lines 3 and 4; and a hasty reading of the poem might tempt us to take the phrase in the sense that man can only look on the Divine light when it is mercifully shrouded. Yet this cannot be the intended meaning since there is nothing to correspond with it in the simile; and even if—to entertain a far-fetched interpretation of the figure—Vaughan was thinking of the moon as reflected sunlight, which the glow-worm could thereby 'face', this reading would not explain 'as glow-worms *shine*'. What ideas, hermetical or otherwise, Vaughan may have held about the light of glow-worms it is hard to say. But in *The Lamp* (ll. 2–4) he seems to be suggesting that the glow-worm's illumination is a form of magnetic 'star-

---

[1] It is just possible that 'veil', along with 'shrine' and 'drawn o'er Thy glorious noon', may have carried some subconscious and imagistic recollection of Luke 23. 45 : 'And the sun was darkened, and the veil of the temple was rent in the midst.'

fire';[1] and on the face of it the conception in lines 3 and 4 of *The Night* is one of glow-worms deriving their light from the moon. They shine because they 'face' the moon: when the moon has gone, their light is dead. In the same way men, worms[2] also in their insignificance, 'live' only when they look upon the 'glorious noon' and sun of Christ.

The second stanza consists mainly of a straightforward development of ideas already present in the opening. In the first place, the image of the 'glorious noon' in the night-time is repeated—a most effective climax to the stanza—in the form of a bold, concentrated paradox, one that is fairly common in religious verse of the time[3] and is to be found elsewhere in Vaughan's writing:[4]

> Did at midnight speak with the Sun!

In the second place, the revelation granted to Nicodemus of the divine in Christ is paralleled and supported by an earlier prophecy of the coming of the Messiah, for the phrase, 'long-expected healing wings,' is a quotation from Malachi 4. 2: 'But unto you that fear my name shall the Sun of righteousness arise with healing in his wings.'[5] This allusion also serves to emphasise the blindness of Nicodemus' fellow-Jews.

[1] *To the Pious Memory of C.W.*, ll. 10–12, contains a similar association, though not a logical connection, between stars and glow-worms. Sir Thomas Browne hints strongly of the same idea. Writing of glow-worms he says: 'Now whether the light of animals, which do not occasionally shine from contingent causes, be not of kin unto the light of heaven; whether the invisible flame of life received in a convenient matter, may not become visible, and the diffused etherial light make little stars by conglobation in idoneous parts of the *compositum*; whether also it may not have some original in the seed and spirit analogous unto the element of stars, whereof some glimpse is observable on the little refulgent humour, at the first attempts of formation; philosophy may yet enquire' (*Pseudodoxia Epidemica*, III. 27 —p. 370, vol. I, *Bohn* ed.).

[2] A felicity of the glow-worm simile is that it fuses the conventional description of man as worm into the dominant imagery of the poem.

[3] See, for example, the line, 'To see another Sun, at midnight rise,' in Giles Fletcher's poem *Christ's Victory and Triumph*.

[4] See *The Dawning*, ll. 5–6, and *The Mount of Olives* (*Works*, p. 169): 'he that sets forth at midnight will sooner meet the Sun than he that sleeps it out betwixt his curtains.'

[5] As the quotation in *The Mount of Olives* (*Works*, p. 151) shows, Vaughan understood Malachi 4. 2 to refer to the coming of Christ.

Through this particular episode of Nicodemus' encounter with Christ Vaughan also introduces the main general theme of this poem, that of night as a blessed and special time of revelation, 'when spirits their fair kindred catch'. Further, linking the first stanza with the last, we may regard the very darkness of night as a necessary condition for the full manifestation of the Divine glory. Yet at the same time the opening communicates something of Vaughan's ambivalent attitude towards the hours of darkness, for his description of Christ as a 'glorious noon' and a 'Sun' cannot but call up the idea of a 'night' that is his hateful, alienating opposite, while the phrase 'glorious noon' seems to require for its implied, antithetical complement the hermetic notion of the 'night of the body'.[1] If these are tenuous, questionable suggestions, there is certainly no missing the association of night with spiritual blindness and apathy in stanza 3 or with death and inanimation in the second line of stanza 4.

On the other hand, the predominant note is one of fundamental, joyous optimism that in the end light will always triumph over darkness, life over death, communion with God over alienation—the assured, jubilant faith that Vaughan elsewhere expresses through such cognate lines and imagery as

> O beamy book! O my midday,
> Exterminating fears and night!

The Agreement

or

> Thy bright arm, which was my light
> And leader through thick death and night!

Abel's Blood

Further, we shall not be falsifying the poem in any way if we sense in his ecstatic account of Nicodemus' revelation something of his own yearning for communion with the Divine light. That is another satisfying link between the beginning and the end of the lyric.

The second movement of the poem, clearly distinguished from

[1] This phrase, used by Thomas Vaughan in *Anthroposophia Theomagica* and *Coelum Terrae*, is Mirandola's.

the first, turns from the image of Christ as the midnight Sun to a fairly simple expression of one of Vaughan's favourite imaginings that may, somewhere about this time, have inspired a complete poem[1]—Christ's vigils of prayer and meditation on the Mount of Olives and in other desolate places.

The writing in this section is unmistakable Vaughan. There is the bold and entirely characteristic image of Christ as a flowering plant,[2] while the lines

> Where trees and herbs did watch and peep
> And wonder, while the Jews did sleep,

present his familiar conception of an intent Creation, the Lord's 'own living works', contrasted as usual with errant man—'sleep' in the above quotation no doubt signifying spiritual lethargy. At the same time this second movement has one or two noticeable weaknesses. Not to stress Vaughan's failure to evoke any really memorable scene (which some readers may feel uncalled for in the context), the third stanza is somewhat mechanical and a trifle monotonous rhythmically in its three, two-line cadences, while the section as a whole is thin and diffuse. It is here that we have the clearest example of one of the waves curling back upon itself, for the question that stanza 3 raises carries its own answer, so that much of stanza 4 comes close to redundancy.

What saves the fourth stanza—if that is not too niggardly a way of describing Vaughan's most successful stroke—is the suggestive impact of the first two lines, the reference to Solomon's temple[3] and the complex, significant contrast that this reference produces. At the level of sensuous impression the bare 'solitary' ground of Christ's ministration is emphasised by contrast with the magnificence of the temple (no doubt more richly and immediately accessible to Vaughan's Bible-schooled readers than

---

[1] *The Dwelling-Place*, though this does not treat specifically of Christ's night-time lodging.

[2] See *St Mary Magdalen*, l. 31, with its image of Christ as a 'green tree'.

[3] The parallel with the overt description of Solomon's temple in *The Palm Tree*, ll. 10–12, the echo in both passages of Herbert's poem *Sion*, and the 'mercy-seat of gold' (Exodus 25. 17)—the golden covering for God's resting-place on the Ark of the Covenant—all establish this reference beyond any doubt.

to ourselves). Here the word 'gold', the only direct indication of colour in the whole poem, stands out most strikingly against the darkness and necessary colourlessness of the scene in the preceding stanza. Along with this comparison we also have the telling juxtaposition of the old, and now dead, dispensation with the new, the supersession of the 'Law' by the 'Gospel'—to quote from the title of an earlier poem entirely devoted to this theme. This second contrast may explain the slightly contemptuous tone of 'dead and dusty' (though this may be an echo from Herbert's *Sion*);[1] and it is just possible, too, that 'carv'd stone' refers to the Tables of the Law, 'all that e'er was writ in stone' (*Man's Fall and Recovery*).

Two further aspects of this allusion call for some brief comment. First, whether Vaughan was himself conscious of this delicate link or not, his use of the phrases 'Virgin shrine' and 'sacred veil' in the first stanza prepares us for the development in stanza 4, once we are intimately familiar with the poem, that is; and it is certainly a legitimate implication to read into the fourth stanza the idea that Christ is his own temple, needing no temple made with hands. The second point, closely linked with the first, is the possibility that the stanza originally carried a special overtone, now lost, in that Vaughan was reassuring himself and his fellow Anglicans not to be unduly perturbed by the closing of their churches. Several of the poems in *Silex Scintillans* bear references (most of them, admittedly, more explicit than the one suggested here) to contemporary religious conditions, and such an allusion would be another reason for Vaughan's deprecatory description of the temple.

On the other hand, however much superficial impression may incline us to this reading, we must not interpret stanza 4 as an expression of the modern belief that God may be worshipped as truly in the countryside as in church. Deep as Vaughan's regard for Nature was, it never betrayed him into this heresy.

[1] *Sion*, ll. 7–8 and 19–20. One of Herbert's basic, and Protestant, ideas was that the essential dwelling-place of God is the human soul. For a similar sentiment in Vaughan's poetry, see *To the Pious Memory of C.W.*, ll. 14–18.

Among the attributes of night, heaped up in stanza 5, there is the line,

> Christ's progress, and His prayer-time.

This, and obviously the opening apostrophe, serve as a sufficient thread of continuity between the third movement and the preceding part of the poem. But the connection is slight and merely formal; and from the fifth stanza onwards, with a very perceptible transition, the poem changes considerably in both character and intensity. Nicodemus and Christ of the vigils on the Mount of Olives disappear. Vaughan is now concerned, in a directly personal way, with his own soul and God; and in this relationship night, significantly re-introduced with the epithet 'Dear', wholly desirable, takes on a new and profound meaning. It becomes, for the first time, the predominant theme of the poem.

However, for all their seriousness and personal urgency, the last two movements of the poem do not immediately rise to their full intensity. The fifth stanza, with its strong alliterations, its short, abrupt cadences, and its approximate though not exact pattern of ascending climax, is certainly emphatic and arresting. Functionally, too, it is most important and effective in the organisation of the poem, for besides linking up, in ways already indicated, with the preceding movements, it announces two of the main themes that are to follow. 'The day of spirits', a phrase adapted from Paracelsus,[1] both recapitulates the poem's fundamental paradox of day-in-night and preludes the following stanza; 'my soul's calm retreat', etc., is to be expanded later into the subject of stanza 8. Nevertheless, the stanza is not altogether a happy one. The artificial, rhetorical construction of the listed attributes (Welsh *dyfalu*, or a common Herbertian and minor Elizabethan sentence-pattern) is out of keeping with the style of the rest of the poem, as is also the intrusion of Vaughan's rougher, more vigorous mode of poetic speech in 'The stop to busy fools'. The last two lines are awkwardly and rather point-

---

[1] 'Paracelsus writes, that the watching of the body is the sleep of the Soul, and that the day was made for corporeal actions, but the night is the working time of spirits' (*Works*, p. 305).

lessly yoked in their rhyming couplet, and the final one is clumsily turned, presumably under the exigency of rhyme and possibly because of the compulsion of an Herbert echo.[1] Again, there are two instances of unintended ambiguity that blunt the impression of the writing. 'The stop to busy fools' may mean that at night foolish men can no longer waste themselves in their fundamentally trivial, worldly business (the most likely interpretation), or it may be the thought, found elsewhere in Vaughan's poetry, that at night he is free from the importunities of other men, even friends and acquaintances. Similarly, the meaning of 'care's check and curb' may be either the restraining of our worldly concerns—the more probable one[2]—or the allaying of our anxieties.

However, these blemishes, revealed more through close familiarity than immediate impression, are not obtrusive; and they are soon overlooked in the strange, haunting beauty of the following stanza, another *dyfalu* but handled with much more rhythmical variation. Here Vaughan is giving sovereign utterance to what was for him the most momentous experience of night and his watches and meditations—the occasional overwhelming sense of divine and angelic presence. There are hints of such communion in *The Mount of Olives*, as when he offers the prayer 'that in the fastest closures of my eyelids my spirit may see Thee, and in the depths of sleep be conversant with Thee',[3] and in *The Search* he writes:

> all night have I
> Spent in a roving ecstasy
> To find my Saviour.

[1] As in *The Morning-Watch*, ll. 17–18, there may have been at work an association between 'prayer' and 'chime' and Herbert's poem *Prayer*—'Church bells beyond the stars heard'.

[2] However, in the Herbert phrase that Vaughan is almost certainly adapting—'care's balm and bay' (*Sunday*)—'care' means worry, anxiety.

[3] *Works*, p. 152. Cf. Bunyan's *Pilgrim's Progress*, part II. After quoting Job 33. 14–16, Bunyan continues: 'We need not, when abed, lie awake to talk with God. He can visit us while we sleep, and cause us then to hear his voice. Our heart ofttimes wakes when we sleep; and God can speak to that, either by words, by proverbs, by signs and similitudes, as well as if one was awake' (*Everyman* ed. pp. 266–7).

There is more than a hint in 'They are all gone into the world of light'—

> And yet, as angels in some brighter dreams
> Call to the soul when man doth sleep.

But this is the fullest and most convincing affirmation of his experience, an experience not of sleep but of wakeful 'dumb watch', of divine as well as angelic visitation; and the poetry quickens to a palpable ecstasy:

> God's silent, searching flight;
> When my Lord's head is filled with dew, and all
> His locks are wet with the clear drops of night;
> His still, soft call;
> His knocking-time. . . .

The striking image of Christ as the lover, urgently searching for his beloved in the night hours, is taken from that richly sensuous love poem, *The Song of Songs*: 'I sleep, but my heart waketh: it is the voice of my beloved that knocketh, saying, Open to me, my sister, my love, my dove, my undefiled: for my head is filled with dew, and my locks with the drops of the night' (5. 2). One of the fullest and most direct of all Vaughan's many Biblical quotations this is also one of his most felicitous—a perfect and appropriate image for his idea, harmonising with his previous picture of Christ; beautifully integrated into the melodic and rhythmical pattern of the poem, so that no one ignorant of the source would guess it to be a quotation; and where altered never impaired but sometimes improved, as in that delicately lingering effect produced by placing 'all' at the end of the second line, isolated from its substantive. 'Dew', following Vaughan's habitual use of the word, almost certainly symbolises divine grace; but, apart from this, there are no subtleties or complexities of meaning in the quotation, which Vaughan no doubt read in the accepted and straightforward allegorical way—the love of Christ for his Church. This quotation also gave Vaughan —by implication—his 'still, soft call' and possibly his 'knocking-time', though behind these phrases there may also have been the echo of two other Biblical texts—'a still small voice' (1 Kings 19. 12), and, 'Behold, I stand at the door, and knock : if any man hear my voice, and open the door, I will come in to him, and will sup with him, and he with me' (Rev. 3. 20). In addition, the first line of the stanza may owe something to a passage in Thomas Vaughan's *Anthroposophia Theomagica* : 'He must be united to the Divine Light. This light descends. . . . I speak of that most secret and *silent lapse of the spirit* "through the degrees of natural forms".'[1]

The stanza also contains several marked echoes of Vaughan himself on other occasions. The opening, for instance, recalls the sentence, 'God pries Through thickest nights', in *Rules and Lessons*, and, even more closely, these lines in *The Feast* :

> How dost Thou fly
> And search and pry
> Through all my parts.

—An odd contradiction perhaps that this wonderful passage should be so derivative. But all Vaughan's borrowings have been stamped with his own individual impress and transmuted into a new whole.

The third and last movements of the poem are very closely connected, so much so that some readers may feel that there is a faulty repetitiveness. Stanza 7 is an obvious elaboration of a phrase in stanza 5—

> my soul's calm retreat
> Which none disturb!

and there is much detailed correspondence between these two stanzas. The key-word 'calm' is repeated; 'unhaunted' (which must mean 'unfrequented') re-echoes the phrase, 'which none disturb'; and 'my loud, evil days' recalls 'busy fools' and pos-

[1] Waite's ed., p. 46. Thomas Vaughan is here discussing regeneration from the Fall.

150

sibly 'cares'. In addition, stanza 7 is directly linked to the preceding stanza by the reference to 'some angel's wing or voice'.

But along with this elaboration there is a new and significant
development of the poem. Always one of Vaughan's deepest and
most characteristic aspirations, at the heart of his spiritual
experience, was his yearning for 'calm' and 'peace' (words that
recur perpetually through his poems)—

> When first I saw True Beauty, and Thy joys
> Active as light, and calm without all noise,
> Shin'd on my soul
>
> *Mount of Olives II*

—and as he meditates on the tranquillity of the 'dark tent'[1] of
night he cannot but feel it to be an intimation of the blessedness
of heaven.[2] This is yet another way in which 'high Heaven'
chimes with the midnight hours.

Throughout stanzas 7 and 8—giving them their continuity—
this new idealisation of night is accentuated by a contrasting condemnation of day, one that is much stronger than anything implied in stanza 5. The sun, evoked here in a significant contrast
with the 'Sun of righteousness' in the first part of the poem, is
an 'ill-guiding light', merely inciting men to all their confused
and sinful worldly activities. The poet's days are described as
'evil', leading him to 'ev'ry mire'. Further, in this description
of earthly life, it is possible that the phrase, 'where all mix and
tire,' originally had a force that is lost to the modern reader.
'Mix' may carry the notion that all created things are mortal
because they are impure mixtures of the elements;[3] while 'tire'
probably alludes to the hermetic belief in the destructive wear-
ing down of the Creation towards its final end—a use of the
word that is also found in the poem, *To I. Morgan*:

---

[1] Vaughan uses this image, or something very much like it, in *The Dwelling-
Place*, ll. 5–7.

[2] Ll. 41–2 may present some difficulty. They might be paraphrased: 'Then I
should always lead a heavenly kind of life and never go astray [as I do] in my
actual mortal life.' 'Keep' means 'dwell' or 'live', not 'insist on remaining'.

[3] Cf. Donne, *The Good-Morrow*, l. 19—'Whatever dies, was not mixt equally.'

So from our cold, rude world, which all things tires,
To his warm Indies the bright sun retires.

The ninth and final stanza, in its undoubted echo from
Dionysius the Areopagite[1]—

There is in God—some say—
A deep, but dazzling darkness

—presents some difficulty in interpretation. Obviously these
lines introduce a further correspondence between night and
heaven and carry the idealisation of night to its extreme limit.
Whereas before Vaughan has been intimating the various
heavenly qualities of night—its peace, its divine visitations—
now he is suggesting that heaven is night, or at least that the
terrestial night prefigures the ultimate mystery of heaven. Yet,
unlike the 'soul's calm retreat' and the 'angel's wing or voice',
this 'deep, but dazzling darkness' is a mystical awareness of God
that Vaughan does not claim to have experienced himself. There
is a notable lack of conviction in his treatment of the experience,
this uncertainty being communicated by his parenthetical *'some
say'* and by his simile of the twilight wayfarers, which, vague
and obscure as it is in some respects,[2] undoubtedly suggests
wavering and dubious perception. Further—not of course to
deny that poets, visionaries, and mystics may entertain diverse,
and even conflicting, images of heaven—Vaughan's much more

[1] Vaughan may have come across Dionysius' description of the Godhead from first-hand reading or through his brother's *Lumen de Lumine*—
'That which is above all degree of intelligence is a certain infinite, inaccessible fire
or light. Dionysius calls it Divine Darkness, because it is invisible and incompre-
hensible' (Waite's ed., p. 269). He may also have remembered some lines in
Herbert's *Even-Song*:

But Thou art Light and darkness both together :
If that be dark we cannot see,
The sun is darker than a tree,
And Thou more dark than either.

[2] One of the difficulties of the simile is to decide the referents of its various
terms. Presumably 'it is late and dusky' corresponds (as a saying) with 'There is
in God. . . . A deep, but dazzling darkness', though it is hard to find any significance for the idea of lateness. 'See not all clear' must mean 'see not entirely clear'.
However, obscure or not, the image is characteristic Vaughan.

usual conception of the Godhead is one of full radiance,[1] as in these lines from *Dressing*,

> Give me, my God! Thy grace,
> The beams and brightness of Thy face.

Can it be that mere play with an idea, a kind of metaphysical ingenuity, has momentarily taken control? that there is a manufactured quality about these lines, and that something of the organic impulse and life of the poem, its intensity and seriousness, has gone?

However, even if justified, adverse criticism must not be pressed too strongly, for the lines certainly serve to concentrate and recapitulate all the main themes of the poem—the image and the paradox of light in darkness, the night-heaven correspondence, and even the earlier experience of Nicodemus, repeated, so to speak, at a heavenly level. Also, by a poetic logic at any rate, they allow Vaughan to close his meditation[2] with an authentic and convincing outcry that has been pressing for utterance through the last two stanzas—his longing to be absorbed inconspicuously[3] in his soul's origin, in the Divine light of the Godhead:

> O for that Night! where I in Him
> Might live invisible and dim!

Though the main purpose of this study of *The Night* has been interpretative, it should have done something to bring out the poem's admirable continuity and articulation.

---

[1] On the other hand, as B. T. Stewart points out ('Hermetic Symbolism in Vaughan's "The Night"', *Philological Quarterly*, vol. XXIX, no. 4, Oct. 1950, p. 418): 'the conception of God as manifesting himself through light springing from infinite and impenetrable darkness is common in Neoplatonic thought, and is almost universal in the work of Renaissance humanists.'

[2] In its structure *The Night* might be regarded as another example of seventeenth-century meditation as expounded by Martz. Stanzas 1-4 would constitute the composition—a strong visualisation of a Bible text; stanzas 5-9 the analysis; and the last two lines of the poem the colloquy.

[3] This is surely one of the meanings of 'invisible and dim'—the sentiment of *Tears, The Throne*, etc.

This feature is worth special notice if only because so much criticism of Vaughan has regularly stressed his constructional weakness, even on the lyric scale—his petering out after some fine opening, his discursiveness, his jolting, zig-zag fits and starts, his inability to end a poem at the right moment.

Applied to his work as a whole, this conventional judgment is a fair one. But it bears little truth in relation to his greatest poems like *The Night*, especially once we have come to appreciate that their mode of evolution is imagistic rather than logical. Further, an appreciation of this point should make us look twice at the more sweeping strictures that are sometimes levelled against the construction of some of his best pieces of the second rank, lyrics like *Cock-Crowing* and *The Timber*.

CHAPTER IX

'THEY ARE ALL GONE INTO THE WORLD OF LIGHT'

They are all gone into the world of light!
 And I alone sit ling'ring here;
Their very memory is fair and bright,
 And my sad thoughts doth clear.

It glows and glitters in my cloudy breast,   5
 Like stars upon some gloomy grove,
Or those faint beams in which this hill is dress'd,
 After the sun's remove.

I see them walking in an air of glory,
 Whose light doth trample on my days: 10
My days, which are at best but dull and hoary,
 Mere glimmering and decays.

O holy Hope! and high Humility,
 High as the heavens above!
These are your walks, and you have show'd them me,   15
 To kindle my cold love.

Dear, beauteous Death! the jewel of the just,
 Shining nowhere, but in the dark;
What mysteries do lie beyond thy dust,
 Could man outlook that mark!   20

He that hath found some fledg'd bird's nest, may know
* At first sight, if the bird be flown;*
But what fair well or grove he sings in now,
* That is to him unknown.*

And yet, as angels in some brighter dreams   25
* Call to the soul when man doth sleep,*
So some strange thoughts transcend our wonted themes,
* And into glory peep.*

If a star were confin'd into a tomb,
* Her captive flames must needs burn there;*   30
But when the hand that lock'd her up, gives room,
* She'll shine through all the sphere.*

O Father of eternal life, and all
* Created glories under Thee!*
Resume Thy spirit from this world of thrall   35
* Into true liberty.*

Either disperse these mists, which blot and fill
* My perspective still as they pass;*
Or else remove me hence unto that hill
* Where I shall need no glass.*   40

ONE feature that the poem 'They are all gone into the world of light' notably shares with *The Morning-Watch* and *The Night* is its exceptionally quintessential quality. It is the gem of a distinctive group of elegies that bear many close resemblances in ideas and phrasing; it expresses, no poem more memorably, Vaughan's intense and continuous yearning for the illumination of heaven and the end of this mist-obscured mortal life; and it is the most concentrated impression he has left us of his light-obsessed imagination.

To consider the lyric a little more closely, we notice that the leading image of the first half, that of the saintly dead as stars or beams guiding us to the 'world of light' (a phrase that epitomises all Vaughan's visions of heaven) occurs in several other poems, most obviously in 'Joy of my Life':

> Joy of my life while left me here!
> And still my Love!
> How in thy absence thou dost steer
> Me from above. . . .
>
> God's saint are shining lights. . . .

And, along with this poem, we may also recall Vaughan's description of his dead wife as 'Fair and young light', his metaphor of the 'solitary lamp' in 'Silence and stealth of days' for the memory of his dead brother, and his lines on St Mary Magdalen's eyes that

> now are fixèd stars, whose light
> Helps such dark stragglers to their sight.

The second stanza is especially rich in reminiscence, for besides the interesting instance of the recurrent cloud–star association,[1] there are also two fairly close verbal parallels to be found. *White Sunday* contains the lines,

> And yet, as in Night's *gloomy* page
> One silent *star* may interline,[2]

and the phrase 'cloudy breast', which may be an echo of the Herbert line, 'They shall be thick and cloudy to my breast' (*Confession*), is exactly repeated in *Easter-Day*.[3] It is also interesting to notice that in both 'They are all gone into the world of light' and *Easter-Day* the phrase 'cloudy breast' is immediately followed by a reference to the sun.

---

[1] See pp. 24–6.   [2] My italics.
[3] *Man in Darkness, Works*, p. 180, also has the phrase 'gloomy breasts'.

However, neither of these correspondences is so remarkable as that between stanza 5—

> Dear, beauteous Death! the jewel of the just,
> Shining nowhere, but in the dark;
> What mysteries do lie beyond thy dust,
> Could man outlook that mark

—and the elegy on his wife, 'As Time one day', where, after several images of light shining—notably in the line, 'Where youth shines like a star'—Vaughan writes,

> Here slept my thought's *dear mark*! which *dust*
> Seem'd to devour....[1]

and, a little later,

> O calm and sacred bed, where lies
> In death's dark mysteries
> A beauty far more bright....

Allowing for certain inevitable commonplaces about death, we can hardly doubt that Vaughan's experience has crystallised into a complex of words and images that is repeated from one poem to the other—whichever was composed first.

Stanza six, again, is extremely characteristic. To say nothing of Vaughan's general interest in birds, *Begging II* (ll. 19–20) contains a substantial simile dealing with the bird's nest and *The Pilgrimage* (ll. 17–20) another long simile of the captive bird's longing for freedom, while there are some lines in one of Vaughan's translations from Boethius that have some correspondence with those in stanza 6:

> Yet, if from her close prison she
> The shady groves doth chance to see,
> Straightway she loathes her pleasant food,
> And with sad looks longs for the wood.
> The wood, the wood alone she loves!
>
> Lib. III, Metrum II

Further, when Vaughan turns to fancies of the fledged bird's destination he calls up two of his favourite details of Old Testa-

---

[1] My italics.

ment landscape, the grove and the well, which appear together in several poems.

With its image of the star descended from its sphere, stanza 8 is yet another passage vibrant with recollections. Nearest to it are the two following passages, the first from *Ascension Hymn* (which, immediately preceding 'They are all gone' in the text of *Silex Scintillans*, may therefore have been written about the same time), and the second from *The Bird*:

[1]
If a star
Should leave the sphere,
She must first mar
Her flaming wear,
And after fall; for in her dress
Of glory she cannot transgress.

[2]
For each enclosèd spirit is a star
Enlight'ning his own little sphere,
Whose light, though fetch'd and borrowèd from far,
Both mornings makes and evenings there.

We may also recollect one of the lines in *The Incarnation and Passion*—'And clothe the morning star with dust'—as well as those remoter, though certainly cognate passages in two other poems:

[1]
A heap of ashes, where some said
A small bright sparkle was a-bed,
Which would one day—beneath the pole—
Awake, and then refine the whole.

The Search

[2]
Did a star,
Beckon'd by Thee, though high and far,
In sparkling smiles haste gladly down
To lodge light. and increase her own?

The Dwelling-Place

159

The dream Angels of stanza 7 recall both the 'angel's wing or voice' in *The Night* and a passage in *The Agreement*:

> At length my life's kind angel came,
> And with his bright and busy wing
> Scatt'ring that cloud. . . .

while the opening of the last stanza,

> Either disperse these mists, which blot and fill
> My perspective still as they pass,

runs very close to some lines in the much earlier *Resurrection and Immortality* (though these lines contain a much more deliberate reference to 1 Cor. 13. 13):

> Then I that here saw darkly in a glass
> But mists, and shadows pass. . . .

If, in its strong distillation quality, 'They are all gone into the world of light' resembles *The Morning-Watch*, *The Night*, and *Regeneration*, in another important respect it is sharply distinguished from these poems. Embodying one predominant, uncomplicated theme, that of Vaughan's longing for heaven as it is stirred in him by his thought of dead friends and relations, sensuous and emotional rather than intellectual in impact, drawing little on hermetic or esoteric ideas, almost devoid of echoes, quotations, and allusions, fairly simple in construction and, for the most part, limpidly written, the poem presents little difficulty of understanding, and there are only two or three stanzas that call for any interpretative comment.

One of these must be the third, which Professor Kermode has instanced as an example of Vaughan's favourite image of the dead as stars. Certainly this image is present, though in an indirect simile form, in the second stanza. But it can have nothing to do with the third, partly because in Vaughan's usual treatment of it the star-dead are fixed, guiding lights—they do not 'walk' —and partly because starlight, which merely 'glows and glitters', would not fit in with the force of 'glory' and 'trample'. The 'glory' and 'light' in which the dead walk is the radiance of heaven, and the following stanza very clearly repeats this idea.

Stanza six may to some extent have been randomly suggested to Vaughan during composition by a dim recollection of some lines in Herbert's *Death*:

> We look'd on this side of thee, shooting short;
> Where we did find
> The shells of fledged souls left behind.[1]

But whether some of its inspiration originated in this way or not, the stanza must not be read as a loosely relevant simile, for it is closely and organically linked with the rest of the poem through the traditional symbol of the winged bird for the soul. It is easy enough, Vaughan is saying, to know when the soul ('hatched' by the love of Christ we might legitimately add, for this conception is the poet's own)[2] has departed from the body, just as it is obvious when the fledged bird has deserted its nest. What puzzles us is where the bird and the soul have gone.

The eighth stanza, beautiful as it is in isolation, may present some difficulty because of its position in the development of the poem (a matter to be discussed later). But its imagery is fairly straightforward. 'Tomb' stands for the body and 'star' for the soul or original divine light (star-fire) in the soul. In addition, taking into account Vaughan's fondness for symbolising Christ as a star and noting the perhaps significantly capitalised 'Tomb' in the first edition, we might just possibly read the stanza as an intimation of the Resurrection, an overtone that would certainly be highly relevant to the poem.

On what grounds does this lyric warrant the high estimation that has usually been given to it?

First, surely, for its concentrated and perfect expression of that intense fascination for light which, common though it is to

---

[1] The first line of the Herbert quotation may also have had some connection with the last line of stanza 5 in Vaughan's poem—'Could man outlook that mark.'
[2] See *Disorder and Frailty* (ll. 47–8) and *Holy Scriptures* (ll. 3–4).

the seventeenth century[1] and to hermetic and Christian meditative writing,[2] remains so exceptionally characteristic of
Vaughan's poetry. There is no other short poem in the language
more brightly and continuously luminous. From the dazzling
impact of its opening line, through images that interpenetrate,
are modified, and are sometimes repeated, it evokes the earthly,
visible light of sunset, stars, and jewels (produced, according to
hermetic theory, by the action of the sun), the strange radiance
of 'some brighter dreams', visited by shining Angels, the divine,
ultimate light, kindling as well as illuminating, that links life
and death, heaven, the departed spirits, and the human soul.
And all this pervasive luminosity is emphasised by Vaughan's
typical, Rembrandtesque chiaroscuro—of stars against 'some
gloomy grove', of the heavenly 'world of light' over and against
the dull glimmering of mortal life, and, most striking of all, of
light in darkness, light triumphant over darkness, at the moment
of death:

> Dear, beauteous Death! the jewel of the just,
> Shining nowhere, but in the dark.

Secondly, for its music, this lyric is undoubtedly one of the
most attractive of Vaughan's major poems.

Not that there is much for special commendation in its rhythmical achievement. Certainly there are numerous pleasing contra-

---

[1] Rosemary Freeman (*English Emblem Books*, p. 124) reminds us of 'the symbolism of darkness and light which so much preoccupied seventeenth century
minds'. There is an interesting passage in Thomas Vaughan's *Aula Lucis* that
probably runs very close to his brother's ideas: 'We see there is a certain face of
light in all those things which are very dear or very precious to us. For example,
in beauty, gold, silver, pearls, and in everything that is pleasant or carries with it
any opinion of happiness—in all such things I say there is inherent a certain secret
concomitant lustre, and whiles they last the possessors also are subject to a clear-
ness and serenity of mind. On the contrary, in all adversity there is a certain cor-
roding, heavy sadness, for the spirit grieves because he is eclipsed and overcast
with darkness. We know well enough that poverty is but obscurity, and certainly
in all disasters there is a kind of cloud, or something that answers to it' (Waite's
ed., pp. 331–2).
[2] Apropos of the imagery of light in St Bonaventura's *Itinerarium Mentis in
Deum*, L. L. Martz remarks that it 'once again reminds us that the fundamental
inspiration for Vaughan's finest achievement does not lie in the occult but in the
great central meditative traditions' (*The Poetry of Meditation*, p. 152).

puntal variations against the basic 5–4–5–3 foot and stress pattern—some of these no doubt fortuitously produced by changes
in accentuation during the years. The poem opens with such a
line,

> They are all gone into the world of light;

and, for an even more striking diversity, there are the lines,

> If a star were confin'd into a tomb,
>   Her captive flames must needs burn there.

Again, the rhythm has at least certain negative merits. Thanks
to the variation of his syntax and construction, Vaughan avoids
the mechanical sing-song that sometimes overtakes him when he
chooses to write in a simple and regular metrical form that
allows no scope for his natural and fluent speech rhythms. He
also escapes the potential danger of his fourth, shortened line—
a monotonous hammer-beat of emphasis, climax, finality; and
even the least sensitive ear should have no difficulty in appreciat-
ing the difference in rhythmic value between, say, 'She'll shine
through all the sphere' and 'Into true liberty'. The rhyming also,
though sometimes weak, is rarely forced.

On the other hand, there is little of the vitality, invention, or
suggestiveness of rhythm that is to be found, sporadically at any
rate, in *The Morning-Watch*, *The Night*, or the opening of *The
Waterfall*.

It is in the poem's sound texture that its musical appeal chiefly
lies. Admittedly this is never particularly rich or subtle. One or
two instances apart—'glows' and 'grove' in stanza two, 'confin'd' and 'shine' in stanza eight—there is no chiming or patterning of vowels; while one of the few repetitions, 'O holy
Hope', is lamentable. But, from the first stanza to the last, the
poem is filled with one of the loveliest of speech sounds, the *l*
consonant, always a favourite to Vaughan's Welsh ear. Most of
the key-words of the poem—'light', 'ling'ring', 'glory', 'love',
'humility', 'walks', 'angels', 'holy', 'soul', 'liberty', 'thrall',
'glass'—carry this alliteration, while it determines many of the
outstanding phrases, like 'glows and glitters', 'call to the soul',

and 'world of thrall'. Yet with all this predominance of a single sound there is no monotony. It comes and goes with varying intensity, rarely again so prominent as it is in the six opening lines, which establish the melody; much of it occurs in the delicate internal form; and it is pleasantly crossed and diversified with numerous minor alliterations, as for example in the lines,

> It glows and glitters in my cloudy breast,
> Like stars upon some gloomy grove.

As with most of even Vaughan's finest lyrics, the expression is by no means faultless. There are one or two traces of flabbiness, like 'And my sad thoughts doth clear', with its forced inversion and line-filling auxiliary verb; and now and then there is something close to redundancy—'fair and bright', 'blot and fill' (which might possibly be justified on melodic grounds), and, more extensively, the lines,

> My days, which are at best but dull and hoary,
> Mere glimmering and decays.

'Trample' (l. 10) has been enthusiastically commended by Miss Mahood[1] as an instance of a Welshman's bold and original handling of English, but in spite of this endorsement many of us are likely to feel that the connotations of the word—gross physical solidity, clumsy ponderous action, etc.—are out of keeping with the associations of 'light'.

However, these minor defects are completely outweighed by the characteristic merits of Vaughan's poetic diction at its best—simplicity and concreteness, a purity difficult to demonstrate but partly to be felt in the freedom from cliché, and a vigorous directness of phrasing. This directness gives the poem a fine start, with a most memorable opening line. Nothing is wasted in preliminaries; and a short main clause of plainest words and basic syntactical pattern, including within itself a phrase of packed suggestion—'world of light', plunges us straight into the central theme and imagery of the poem. This quality of phrasing is notably present in several other stanzas, in such

---

[1] *Poetry and Humanism*, p. 254.

expressions as 'kindle my cold love', 'captive flames', and 'hand that lock'd her up'; while all through the piece, sustaining its vigour, main clauses predominate over subsidiary ones.

There are also one or two instances of Vaughan's effective fusion of the concrete and abstract—

> I see them walking in an air of glory. . . .

and

> And into glory peep

Possibly 'peep' in the middle of the seventeenth century was entirely, or relatively, free of furtive, prurient, and comic associations. But, if we may judge this line by a purely twentieth-century response, the combination of 'glory' and 'peep' is a bold and hazardous one that just—only just—succeeds.

In its organisation, on the other hand, the poem is decidedly inferior to *The Morning-Watch* and *The Night*. It begins well— four necessary, close-linked stanzas that rise urgently to the impressive climax of 'Dear, beauteous Death', etc., in stanza five. 'Mysteries' in this same stanza suggests that the development of the poem might turn on something of a contrast, the hopes, the assurances of 'glory', weighed to some extent against the unknown. Indeed, the following stanza on the fledged bird's nest does begin to develop this contrast; but in stanza seven, and still more in stanza eight, we are switched back to the intimations and assurance of heavenly glory, with the result that we have a sense of lost or arrested pattern and even of some obscurity in an otherwise transparent poem.

More serious still, the last two stanzas are very repetitive in sentiment and idea. What the poem calls out for in conclusion is something much more compact, a firm and memorable compression of these eight slackly phrased and sometimes prosaic lines. Their sentiment is deep and authentic Vaughan: no question about that; but somehow the pith, the poetic vitality, has gone out of the writing. Once again, and this time in one of his greatest lyrics, we are confronted with the poet who does not know when or how to stop.

PART III

SOME GENERAL IMPRESSIONS

CHAPTER X

FURTHER NOTES ON VAUGHAN'S IMAGERY

In the union of the temporal with the immortal, this world and the world beyond, Vaughan obtains an easy hold upon his reader, and is able to suggest strange and celestial concords by the simplest references to daily experience here.   E. BLUNDEN, *On the Poems of Henry Vaughan*[1]

WE have already examined, in some detail, Vaughan's Nature images and many of those drawn from esoteric sources.[2] But there is another important strand of imagery to be noticed that lends considerable variety to his poetry. Following the example of Herbert,[3] he also turns habitually to everyday and domestic life for his figures and illustrations.

A good instance of this kind of imagery to start with is his occasional reference to some form of domestic illumination, since we may discover here examples of both remote and familiar application of the same material. Thus, along with those obscure uses of 'lamp' that we have previously noticed[4] (and sometimes of 'candle'), we may set, for contrast, his fine and homely simile in 'Joy of my life' for the saints of God:

> But these all night,
> Like candles, shed
> Their beams, and light
> Us into bed.

[1] S. L. Bethell, *The Cultural Revolution of the Seventeenth Century*, p. 136, makes a similar comment: 'his style is full of imagery drawn from a variety of sources: nature, town life, science, the ordinary domestic round. Thus, although his theme is remote from the everyday, material world, that world is none the less present in his verse as its explanatory principle: the reader feels himself in the real world.'

[2] Among the esoteric images there is of course the ring of Eternity, mentioned for another purpose on p. 5.

[3] See pp. 51–2.   [4] See p. 124.

In a similar vein there is his more elaborate image in *The Feast* of God as a careful householder searching for patches of unhealthy damp in one of his dwellings :

> How dost Thou fly
> And search and pry
>> Through all my parts, and, like a quick
> And knowing lamp,
> Hunt out each damp,
>> Whose shadow makes me sad or sick!

Among his variants of the 'lamp' metaphor the best is not the one in the poem of that name, a laboured and heavily emblematic piece that never lives up to the promise of its intense, haunting opening, but the image, also fully elaborated, in 'Silence and stealth of days'. As several critics have suggested, his initial treatment of the figure may owe something to Plato's famous analogy, for there is certainly some correspondence :

> As he that in some cave's thick damp,
>> Lock'd from the light,
> Fixeth a solitary lamp
>> To brave the night,
> And walking from his Sun, when past
>> That glimm'ring ray,
> Cuts through the heavy mists in haste
>> Back to his day. . . .

But the bold, resourceful manipulation of the image that follows is entirely his own. Employing it, first, for an urgent and convincing representation of his last recollections, so comforting and assuring, of his dead brother, he then proceeds to a no less effective distinction between the 'beams' and 'snuff' of the now extinct lamp :

> I search, and rack my soul to see
>> Those beams again;
> But nothing but the snuff to me
>> Appeareth plain :
> That, dark and dead, sleeps in its known
>> And common urn;
> But those, fled to their Maker's throne,
>> There shine, and burn.

Here the easy organic unfolding of the image stands out in sharpest contrast with the accumulated contrivances of *The Lamp*.

Another distinct group of references to everyday life includes wayfaring, roads, streets, paths, tracks, etc. Yet though Vaughan's poetry is so individually and pervasively infused with the sentiment of 'the business of a Pilgrim is to seek his country',[1] this does not produce quite the richness of concrete detail we might expect, as we may see from *The Pilgrimage* and *Death I. The World* (in *Thalia Rediviva*) certainly contains a long image of this kind (and one that is reminiscent of a passage[2] in the early *A Rhapsodis*):

> never let me miss
> Nor leave the path which leads to Thee,
> Who art alone all things to me!
> I hear, I see, all the long day
> The noise and pomp of the broad way.
> I note their coarse and proud approaches,
> Their silks, perfumes, and glittering coaches.
> But in the narrow way to Thee
> I observe only poverty,
> And despis'd things; and all along
> The ragged, mean, and humble throng
> Are still on foot; and as they go
> They sigh, and say, their Lord went so.

But most of the allusions of this sort are bare and trite, like the 'foul road'[3] (for life) in 'Joy of my life' and 'this inn And road of sin' in *Christ's Nativity*. *Faith* has the line, 'stars shut up shop', an appropriation from Cleveland's poem *Upon Phillis* that is not very happy in its new context, while *The Ornament* elaborates at some length the metaphor of the world's 'gorgeous mart and glittering store'. On the other hand, this group of images includes two entirely admirable figures—the well-known

> But ah! my soul with too much stay
> Is drunk, and staggers in the way!

---

[1] *The Mount of Olives, Works*, p. 169.   [2] This passage is quoted on p. 191.
[3] Vaughan's order of noun and epithet has been reversed.

in *The Retreat*, and, perhaps an even better one, the striking
and original opening of *The Ass*:

> Thou who didst place me in this busy street
> Of flesh and blood, where two ways meet. . . .

Another group of everyday images, much more prominent
than either of the two so far described, is connected with houses[1]
and domestic activity. Here the most widely recurrent one is the
commonplace of the house (or cottage) for the body, the best
and most sustained example[2] of which is to be found in *Burial*:

> Thou great Preserver of all men!
> Watch o'er that loose
> And empty house,
> Which I sometimes liv'd in.
>
> It is, in truth, a ruin'd piece,
> Not worth Thy eyes;
> And scarce a room but wind and rain
> Beat through, and stain
> The seats and cells within;
> Yet Thou
> Led by Thy love wouldst stoop thus low,
> And in this cot,
> All filth and spot,
> Didst with Thy servant inn.

Closely linked with this image is that of the soul as a room for
the reception of God, the most familiar instance[3] of which is the
conclusion of the favourite anthology piece, *The Dwelling-Place*.
Occasionally, too, Vaughan draws on the outside of the house
for an image. Several times he repeats the Biblical figure of God
knocking at the door; and in *Man* this image (which might of
course be included in the street-wayfaring group) represents the
lost human soul—'He knocks at all doors, strays and roams.'
Admission has a metaphorical reference to rain beating at the

---

[1] This group also includes the curtained bed, discussed on pp. 26–8.

[2] See also *Resurrection and Immortality*, ll. 39–40, and 'Thou that knowst', ll. 14–15.

[3] Cf. *Christ's Nativity*, ll. 19–20, *Dressing*, ll. 4–5, and also *To the Pious Memory of C.W.*, ll. 57–60. The last two of these examples are linked by a common 'key' reference.

windows, while a simile in *L'Envoy* suggests that Vaughan knew from personal experience the disadvantage of living too near a stream:

> For sin—like water—hourly glides
> By each man's door, and quickly will
> Turn in, if not obstructed still.

Images of domestic activity are not numerous, and they are notable only as forming part of the general 'household' group. But they include one of Vaughan's most memorable figures (and one again with Biblical antecedents):

> Man is the shuttle, to whose winding quest
> And passage through these looms
> God order'd motion, but ordain'd no rest.
>
> *Man*

They also reveal his fondness, like Herbert, for illustrating grave themes with the homeliest of details. Among his meditations on his wife's mortal remains are the lines,

> As we for long and sure recruits,
> Candy with sugar our choice fruits;
>
> 'As Time one day'[1]

and in *Dressing*, in a deeply-felt attack on the Puritan attitude to the Communion, he writes:

> Give me, my God! Thy grace . . .
> That never like a beast
> I take Thy sacred feast,
> Or the dread mysteries of Thy blest blood
> Use with like custom as my kitchen food.
>
> Some sit to thee, and eat
> Thy body as their common meat;
> O let me not do so!

One feeling Vaughan did share with the Puritans was apparently a contempt for 'curl'd puff'd points, Or a laced story'.[2] On

---

[1] This fine poem has a good deal of imagery of the kind under discussion—a 'curious book', a 'Kalendar', 'candle-light', a 'bright lamp', etc.

[2] *Content*, ll. 17–18. See also *The Ornament* passim, and, from earlier poetry, *To Lysimachus*, ll. 9–12.

the other hand, beside his two poems on articles of dress—
Content and *Upon a Cloke lent him by Mr J. Ridsley* (the latter
one of the best of his early pieces)—his work reveals a surprising number of metaphors and expressions associated with cloth-
ing. As Blunden has pointed out, he frequently uses 'undressing'
as a synonym for dying—'Who will ascend, must be undrest'[1];
and once, with a rare metaphysical boldness of paradox, he
employs this analogy for the surcease of Death itself:

> Softly rest all thy virgin-crumbs!
> Lapp'd in the sweets of thy young breath,
> Expecting till Thy Saviour comes
> To dress them, and unswaddle death.

> *The Burial of an Infant*

This quotation also contains the complement of his 'undressing'
metaphor—the figure of 'dressing' to denote the assumption
either of immortality or a state of special spirituality. In *Resurrection and Immortality*, his usual Puritanism forgotten, he tells
how the dead body

> Like some spruce bride,
> Shall one day rise, and cloth'd with shining light,
> All pure and bright,
> Re-marry to the soul;

and in *Praise*, with the alternative use of this image, he declares
how even in this life

> my soul in new array
> I will dress Thee.

In *The Incarnation and Passion*, using 'undress' in the more
common way, he writes (with a strong Herbert reminiscence)[2]:

> Lord, when Thou didst Thyself undress,
> Laying by Thy robes of glory....

But though the 'robes of glory' belong to Christ in heaven,
Vaughan's imagination appears to have been caught by the
Biblical descriptions[3] of Christ's shining raiment on earth. The

---

[1] *Ascension Hymn*, l. 6. See also *Vanity of Spirit*, ll. 33–4 and 'Fair and Young
Light', l. 48.
[2] See *The Bag*, ll. 9–12. [3] Matthew 17. 2; Mark 9. 3; Luke 9. 29.

image of the second Dedication poem—

> As Thy clothes, when Thou with clothes were clad,
> Both light from Thee, and virtue had—

reappears dramatically in *Ascension Hymn* as

> Then comes He!
> Whose mighty light
> Made His clothes be
> Like heav'n, all bright.

Parallel with this[1] is the commonplace of the Church, Christ's spouse, attired in her 'seamless coat', 'her perfect and pure dress'.[2]

At other times, possibly in consequence of his own indifference to fine clothes, his visualisation of ideas turns to images of rags, tears, and stains. In the second Dedication poem men—or perhaps their physical bodies—are described as 'poor rags', in *Ascension Hymn* as 'garments . . . dark and spoil'd'; and in *L'Envoy* he admits how the 'seamless coat' of the Church 'is grown a rag'. In *White Sunday* he vehemently concentrates all his contempt for the Puritan distortion of true doctrine in the line, 'And on Christ's coat pin all their shreds.' *The Constellation* concludes with the prayer that God will 'repair these rents' in the 'perfect and pure dress' of the Church. But none of these phrases is so memorable as the close and probably deliberate echo of Heb. 1. 11–12 in *L'Envoy*—an outstanding example of Vaughan's fusion of the daily domestic commonplace with his deepest religious aspirations:

> Arise, arise!
> And like old clothes fold up these skies,
> This long-worn veil.

The third line of this quotation contains another recurrent image, which, even if it is not strictly connected with dress, may

---

[1] Note also the allusion in *The Book*, ll. 7–8, to the linen in which the crucified body of Christ was wrapped.

[2] 'Her perfect and pure dress' occurs in *The Constellation*, l. 57. The *British Church*, l. 8, and *L'Envoy*, l. 30, contain 'seamless coat', a phrase which may have come to Vaughan from Herbert's *Divinity*, l. 11. In *White Sunday* 'Christ's coat', l. 14, must refer to the Church.

be briefly[1] mentioned here. Though used in a variety of contexts, 'veil' most frequently symbolises the physical body or the physical world; and in the line just quoted both meanings are probably present. To some extent the symbol may be regarded as given, and indeed commonplace, for it is prominent in the Bible,[2] in hermetic writing, and in the Emblem books. But because it is used to express one of the most persistent themes of his poetry—his sense of the frustration of mortal life and of the severance between man and God—it is also a highly characteristic Vaughan word, stamping with his signature such lines as the seventh stanza of *Cock-Crowing*:

> Only this veil which Thou hast broke,
> And must be broken yet in me,
> This veil, I say, is all the cloak
> And cloud which shadows Thee from me.
> This veil Thy full-ey'd love denies,
> And only gleams and fractions spies.

One further group of everyday images is made up of medical references.[3] This group is a sizeable one and has often been noted, partly because it is involved in the biographical problem of when Vaughan first started to practise as a doctor; but it contains little of interest or importance. Most of these images and expressions are concerned with medicines and 'salves and syrups', and—rather generally—with afflictions and diseases, like the 'cancerous, close arts' in *L'Envoy*. There is an unusually

---

[1] Miss Mahood, *Poetry and Humanism*, pp. 262–4, has already discussed this important image fully and admirably. She notes that Vaughan employs it twenty times in his prose and verse.

[2] See especially Hebrews 10. 20, and 2 Corinthians 3. 14–16.

[3] The following list includes most of Vaughan's medical allusions, apart from those quoted in the text: 'Vain wits and eyes', l. 6; *Day of Judgment*, ll. 35–6; *Affliction*, ll. 1–3; *Misery*, ll. 83–4; *White Sunday*, l. 44; *The Proffer*, l. 44; *Cock-Crowing*, l. 32; *Joy*, ll. 5–6; *Childhood*, ll. 14–16; *Righteousness*, l. 30; and *Death*, ll. 21–3. Blunden, who has noted most of these references, also draws attention to three faintly pharmaceutical expressions—'dram' (*The Evening Watch*, l. 5), 'heaven extracted' (*Holy Scriptures*, l. 2), 'extract' and 'wash your vessel well' (*The Sap*, ll. 41–3). Since Blunden's book, R. H. Walters has reminded us (*Henry Vaughan and the Alchemists*, p. 117) that 'balsam' (or 'balm') and 'exhalation' are precise terms from hermetic medicine.

extensive example of this type of imagery in *The Agreement*, one in which God is represented as the Divine Physician:

> for Thou
> Dost still renew, and purge and heal:
> Thy care and love, which jointly flow,
> New cordials, new cathartics deal.

Finally, among the miscellanea, we may notice in such recurrent words as 'perfume', 'odour', 'incense', 'spice', 'myrrh', 'ointment', and 'balm' a fondness for scents and unguents, the several musical allusions[1], the sporadic legal-financial references,[2] and the occasional metaphors relating to suckling,[3] watches and clocks, the perspective-glass (telescope), and books,[4] especially their pages. A typical book image occurs in the lines:

> And yet, as in Night's gloomy page
> One silent star may interline;
>
> *White Sunday*

and a particularly striking one, though lifted straight from Revelation 6. 14, in

> When like a scroll the heavens shall pass
> And vanish clean away.
>
> *Day of Judgment*

In his excellent book, *The Fire and the Fountain*, John Press has these two general comments to make on poetic imagery: 'One of the marks by which we recognise a poet is his ability to stamp the images he uses—no matter what their source—with the indelible mark of his imagination' (p. 194); and 'all . . . will be in vain if the images fail to represent with complete fidelity

---

[1] E.g. *Affliction*, ll. 35–40; *Joy*, ll. 1–10; 'Thou that knowst', ll. 51–2.

[2] See *Dedication I*, l. 14; *Death I*, l. 4; *Son Days*, ll. 18–19; *The Match*, parti ll. 9–10; *Faith*, l. 9; *Death II*, ll. 8–10.

[3] See *Admission*, l. 17; *The Seed Growing Secretly*, ll. 9–10; *Easter Hymn*, ll. 11–12, as well as *Etesia going beyond Sea*, ll. 18–20. This image probably has an Herbert origin—cf. *Longing*, ll. 17–18, *The Holy Scriptures*, ll. 1–2, and the last stanza of *Whitsunday* (in the Williams MS.).

[4] See also, apart from the incidental metaphors elsewhere, *The Book*, and, in *Thalia Rediviva*, *To his Books*.

the private and unique vision which he is trying to delineate' (p. 195).

If we judge the whole of Vaughan's imagery (including the groups discussed in the early part of this book) by these important and searching criteria, he emerges, beyond doubt, as an authentic and considerable poet. Drawn from a variety of sources, sometimes obviously borrowed from other writers, his images are nevertheless almost always signed with his own imagination and sensibility; and they certainly communicate—if on occasions fitfully—a rare individual vision. Further, as we have often seen, his imagery is bound together by a surprising number of recurrent associations that are probably indicative of a great reservoir in him of subconscious inspiration and imaginative life.

It would be unsound to argue that these image-complexes, or the reservoir behind them, are the infallible signs of a great poet. There are certainly many instances to the contrary. But they are frequently found in the work of many outstanding poets—in Shakespeare and Keats, to name two notable examples.

CHAPTER XI

VAUGHAN'S MUSIC

Now and then in his poetry Vaughan will delight us with a passage in which his sound-texture or manipulation of rhythm (or both) have a striking expressive effect: where, that is to say, his music suggests or enacts something of his meaning.

We have already noticed several admirable examples of this kind of writing in our study of four of his major poems. But it is also to be found outside the recognised masterpieces. Consider, for instance, the opening lines of *Unprofitableness*, a poem that, in its intricate chiming of repeated vowels and consonants, its assonances and internal rhymes and half-rhymes, is probably the most musical piece Vaughan ever wrote—in melodic texture, if not in rhythm:

> How rich, O Lord! how fresh Thy visits are!
> 'Twas but just now my bleak leaves hopeless hung
> Sullied with dust and mud;
> Each snarling blast shot through me, and did share
> Their youth, and beauty, cold show'rs nipt, and wrung
> Their spiciness, and blood.

Here, in the second and third lines, the flat, rather muffled *u* vowel that is so closely and markedly repeated in 'just', 'hung', 'sullied', 'dust', and 'mud' (and distantly echoed in 'wrung' and 'blood') effectively suggests a drooping inertness, while the predominance of monosyllables, the aspirates of 'hopeless hung', and the deceleration of line 2 that is produced by the immediately repeated *e* vowel of 'bleak leaves' and the rhythmical weighting of the speech-stresses at the end—'bléak leáves hópe-less húng'—all help to create an impression of heaviness and immobility.

It is perhaps less easy to analyse the effect of the three lines that follow. There is an unmistakable communication of energy and destructive force in the fourth line, in the *sn* of 'snarling', the repeated *sh*, and in the onomatopoeic sound of 'blast', possibly some suggestion of the relentless force of the storm produced by the close, hammered repetitions, all in the space of one line, of 'snarling', 'blast', and 'share',[1] and certainly a very palpable release of rhythmic movement. The phrase, 'cold show'rs nipt', with its contrasting brevity and abruptness, its monosyllables, and, once again, the deceleration of three consecutive speaking stresses, temporarily halts the release. But it is a most apt variation, indicative of the sharp, freezing nature of the storm.

Some of these suggestions may be rather subjective. That is the continual danger of this kind of interpretative criticism. But at least there can be no doubt about the general and most effective contrast in sound and rhythm between the two sections of the passage.

Another passage that is singularly satisfying for its musical expressiveness is the first section of *The Waterfall* (often included in the anthologies, though not quite one of Vaughan's finest poems):

> With what deep murmurs through time's silent stealth
> Doth thy transparent, cool and wat'ry wealth
> > Here flowing fall,
> > And chide, and call,
> As if his liquid, loose retinue stay'd
> Ling'ring, and were of this steep place afraid,
> > The common pass
> > Where, clear as glass,
> > All must descend
> > Not to an end :
> But quick'ned by this deep and rocky grave,
> Rise to a longer course more bright and brave.

Here perhaps the outstanding musical achievement is the suggestion of the pause, the seeming hesitation of the stream before it makes its decisive plunge, that Vaughan creates by his return

---

[1] I am assuming that 'share' was pronounced to rhyme with 'are'.

to long lines in lines 5 and 6, by the unbroken flow of line 5 into line 6 before the emphatic and unexpected arrest after 'ling'ring', and by the weighting and slowing-up of line 6 through the three close, speaking stresses at the end—'steep place afraid'. But there are other felicities, notably the counterpoint effect of the natural, uncontorted word-order and the flowing supple rhythm of one long sentence against the taut and highly formal metrical pattern, the continuous contrast[1] between the long lines for the course of the stream before and after its fall and the shortened lines for its abrupt headlong plunge, and the smoothness of the difficult modulations involved. One example will suffice of Vaughan's deft, assured manipulation of his intricate metrical scheme. The poem begins with a masterly line, which, moving with a grave, unhurried pace, the very rhythm of time over its long expanses, immediately strikes the ear with an impressive depth and resonance.[2] But there is no discordance between this line and the shortened lines that constitute most of the section : first, because the second line, with its lighter vowels and slight acceleration of movement (it has only four speaking stresses), modulates delicately into the shortened third and fourth lines, and secondly, because the third line, short as it is metrically, is weighted and comparatively slow-moving through the length of the vowels—and possibly the alliteration—of 'flowing fall'.

Besides these rare moments of an expressive word music that is an integral part of the experience he is communicating, Vaughan also gives us from time to time (if some puritan, and strictly functional, mid-twentieth century principles do not rule out such simple pleasures of poetry) passages and stanzas of considerable aural beauty arising from the marked repetition

[1] Both Rosemary Freeman (*English Emblem Books*, p. 153) and S. L. Bethell (*The Cultural Revolution of the Seventeenth Century*, p. 150) have noted that on the printed page the first section of *The Waterfall* visually suggests its subject.

[2] These effects are produced by the weightiness of the vowels, particularly the close repetition of the long *i*'s in 'Time's' and 'silent', the six speaking stresses and their proximities—'what deep murmurs' and 'Time's silent stealth', and by the lightness of the pause after 'murmurs' and again at the end of the line.

and interweaving of vowels and consonants. One such is the opening of his mediocre poem *Dressing* :[1]

> O Thou that lovest a pure, and whiten'd soul!
> That feedst among the lilies, till the day
> Break, and the shadows flee; touch with one coal
> My frozen heart; and with Thy secret key
>
> Open my desolate rooms; my gloomy breast
> With Thy clear fire refine, burning to dust
> These dark confusions, that within me nest,
> And soil Thy temple with a sinful rust.

In these lines the sustained, even-pulsed flow of the rhythm is certainly impressive, while Vaughan's continual overriding of the line-endings is a positive achievement of the poem, since it communicates an urgency of utterance. But the very marked sound pattern of the two stanzas—the repeated *o* vowel of 'O', 'shadows', 'coal', etc., the interchanged *e* of 'feedst', 'flee', 'secret', and 'key', the continuous *f* and *l* alliterations, the internal rhyme of 'rooms' and 'gloomy', the sudden piercing *i* vowel of 'fire refine'—is in the main pleasurable rather than suggestive, an accompaniment rather than an expression of meaning or intention.

However, even word music of this sort is comparatively rare in *Silex Scintillans*, and in general the sound-texture of Vaughan's poetry is plain spun, as his rhythm, especially in his favourite octosyllabic measure,[2] is frequently undistinguished, mechanical, and sometimes clumsy. That said, it is perhaps relevant to notice here that the passage just quoted from *Dressing* draws heavily on the Bible and Herbert,[3] for it is quite likely that its exceptional richness of word music was a carry-over from

---

[1] For another good example see the first two stanzas of *The Queer*.

[2] E. Blunden, who calls Vaughan a 'master' of the octosyllabic couplet, adds: 'So long as he is employing octo-syllables his thought advances vigorously and clearly, and is strengthened by apt modification of accent and sound' (*On the Poetry of Henry Vaughan*, p. 46). E. W. Williamson is rightly, I think, more critical: 'his favourite metre is the easy octosyllables, and in that he sometimes flies and sometimes flags' (*Henry Vaughan*, p. 27).

[3] Ll. 2–3 are a quotation from The Song of Songs 4. 5–6; 'fire refine' echoes Malachi 3. 2; and ll. 4–5 are adapted from Herbert's *Holy Communion*, ll. 21–2.

Vaughan's sources and that when the suggestive force of these echoes was spent he lapsed into his more common, plainer style.

One is forced to go further and admit that, so far as poetic melody is concerned, Vaughan had not a very sensitive ear. Even in those passages where he does achieve some pleasing aural effect one often feels that his melodic line was probably created without much contrivance and perhaps without much awareness. And there are certainly moments when his ear is quite defective. How dangerously close, for instance, he comes to destroying the delightful interchange of *i* and *o* vowels and the delicate *l* alliteration of

> their green branches shoot
> Towards the old and still enduring skies,
> While the low violet thrives at their root
>
> *The Timber*

with the jarring collision of 'groves grow' in the immediately preceding phrase.

However, as we have already seen in *The Waterfall*, Vaughan often displays one vital and compelling rhythmical impulse in his poetry. Like so many of the metaphysicals, but more commonly than anyone else except Donne, he frequently creates a dynamic tension in his poems by forcing his predominantly speech rhythms across some fairly elaborate (and, if one likes to use the word, artificial) metrical form of diversified rhyme pattern and line length.

Negatively described, this tension arises from his resistance to the strong mechanical pressure that both his exacting and sometimes intricate rhyme scheme and his often arbitrary variations of line length exert upon his syntax and word-order, his shaping of cadences and placing of pauses. In more positive terms, he gives some potentially rigid, even constricting, metrical form suppleness and motion by freely running his sense across line endings, by employing strong mid-line pauses, and by expressing himself in varied cadences and long sweeps of rhythm extending over many lines, sometimes over an entire stanza.

Often, though not always, this tension between the cross-weaving thread of rhythm and the frame of stanzaic structure is heightened by strong counterpoint between the natural speech stresses and the underlying metrical pulse. Commonly these speaking stresses intensify or weaken the metrical beat, syncopate it, and produce consecutive strong accents. A striking example (though merely one out of many) of this kind of rhythmical effect is to be found in 'As Time one day':

> Where through thick pangs, high agonies
> Faith into life breaks, and death dies.

In particular, as we have already noticed in *The Waterfall* and elsewhere,[1] Vaughan has a marked Keatsian habit of weighting the end of his lines with several closely recurrent stresses.

A comparison of the first two stanzas of *Regeneration*, where the original punctuation serves as a good, though not exact, notation for the pauses, may help in elucidation. In the opening stanza the tension between the urgent, continuous cross-rhythm and the underlying metrical pattern is to be felt most strongly:

> A ward, and still in bonds, one day
> I stole abroad,
> It was high-Spring, and all the way
> Primros'd, and hung with shade;
> Yet, was it frost within,
> And surly winds
> Blasted my infant buds, and sin
> Like clouds eclips'd my mind.

In the second stanza the main rhythmical effect is quite different. Here, especially in the first four lines, Vaughan has allowed his cadences to be shaped, fairly closely, by the dictates of his line lengths and rhymes: every line ends with a definite pause, several of them heavy, and the median pauses are of the slightest:

> Storm'd thus; I straight perceiv'd my Spring
> Mere stage, and show.
> My walk a monstrous, mountain'd thing
> Rough-cast with rocks, and snow;

[1] See the commentary on *The Night*, pp. 140-1.

And as a pilgrim's eye
Far from relief,
Measures the melancholy sky
Then drops, and rains for grief. . . .

Though this second stanza serves for a convenient illustration by opposites, it is an exception, and as a whole *Regeneration* is outstandingly filled with the rhythmical tension we are considering. Besides stanza one there are several others that demonstrate it most unmistakably—the seventh, for one :

Only a little fountain lent
Some use for ears,
And on the dumb shades language spent
The music of her tears;
I drew her near, and found
The cistern full
Of divers stones, some bright, and round
Others ill-shap'd, and dull.

In this passage Vaughan has given great plasticity to the metrical form by continually running his sense from one line into another and by the variously cadenced rhythm that weaves across the last four, where, especially in the very short sixth line, the basic metre might so easily have dominated. Indeed, all through the poem, he vigorously and successfully imposes his own natural rhythms on the powerful mechanical compulsions of the last four lines of each stanza.

There are many other poems (including several of the best) that reveal this compelling tension in some degree—*Resurrection and Immortality*, 'Joy of my Life', *The Morning-Watch*, *Burial*, *The Check*, *Disorder and Frailty*, *Man*, 'I walk'd the other day', 'As Time one day', *The Night*, and, as we have already seen, the opening section of *The Waterfall*. From these we may select three extracts for particular illustrations.

First, for a very close similarity of effect to *Regeneration*, there is the last stanza of *The Check* :

Hark, how He doth invite thee! with what voice
Of love, and sorrow
He begs, and calls; 'O that in these thy days

Thou knew'st but thy own good!'
Shall not the cries of blood,
Of God's own blood awake thee ? He bids beware
Of drunk'ness, surfeits, care,
But thou sleep'st on; where's now thy protestation,
Thy lines, thy love ? Away,
Redeem the day,
The day that gives no observation,
Perhaps to-morrow.

'As Time one day' is remarkable for the urgency with which Vaughan forces his sense, and rhythm, across the considerable counter-pressure of the tight couplet rhyming, notably in the following passage, which also contains, in pleasing contrast with the fluidity of the first two lines, some vigorous and arresting counterpoint and deceleration :

Many disordered lives I saw
And foul records which thaw
My kind eyes still, but in
A fair, white page of thin
And ev'n, smooth lines, like the sun's rays,
Thy name was writ, and all thy days.

Finally, there is the interesting opening of *Resurrection and Immortality*, which, though strongly conditioned in cadence by its somewhat arbitrary variation of line length, and bearing frequent pauses at the end of lines, shows in an exceptional way what can be done to override the basic metrical form by a long, sustained sweep of rhythm :

Oft have I seen, when the renewing breath
That binds, and loosens death
Inspir'd a quick'ning power through the dead
Creatures abed,
Some drowsy silkworm creep
From that long sleep
And in weak, infant hummings chime, and knell
About her silent cell
Until at last full with the vital ray
She wing'd away,

> And proud with life, and sense,
> Heaven's rich expense,
> Esteem'd (vain things!) of two whole elements
> As mean, and span-extents.

Occasionally Vaughan successfully imposes a flexibly vigorous cross-running rhythm on groups of short, close-rhymed lines. We have observed something of this effect in *The Morning-Watch*,[1] and there is an admirable example in 'Joy of my life':

> A swordlike gleam
> Kept man for sin
> First *out*; this beam
> Will guide him *in*.

But in general, as poems like 'Come, come, what do I here?', *Midnight*, *Ascension-Hymn*, and *The Feast* reveal, a metrical scheme of short lines and close rhyming (especially in couplets) precludes that sort of rhythmic tension we are at present considering. In these poems Vaughan's cadences and rhythms are nearly always dictated by the metrical form:

> There's not a wind can stir,
> Or beam pass by,
> But straight I think (though far)
> Thy hand is nigh;
> Come, come!
> Strike these lips dumb:
> This restless breath
> That soils Thy name,
> Will ne'r be tame
> Until in death.
>
> 'Come, come, what do I here?'

This tension we have been examining is one that arises principally when Vaughan is basing his poem on some moderately elaborate stanza form. But the general contrast between music of a predominantly metrical kind and music in which the metre is energetically crossed by fluent, plastic, usually speech rhythms

[1] See p. 127.

is to be observed elsewhere in his poetry. For instance, the form of alternate four- and two-stress lines, rhyming *ababcdcd*, etc., which he uses in a number of poems, is always likely to exert the strongest rhythmic pressure on the writer—even to the point of mechanical monotony—as we may see in *The Pursuit* :

> Hadst Thou given to this active dust
> A state untir'd,
> The lost son had not left the husk
> Nor home desir'd;
> That was Thy secret, and it is
> Thy mercy too,
> For when all fails to bring to bliss,
> Then, this must do.

But, as the following lines from *The Resolve* show, even the compulsions of this metrical form can be profoundly modified by an impassioned utterance of cross-flowing rhythm in which the poet makes bold use of arresting mid-line pauses :

> I have consider'd it; and find
> A longer stay
> Is but excus'd neglect. To mind
> One path, and stray
> Into another, or to none,
> Cannot be love;
> When shall that traveller come home,
> That will not move ?

Adding to the rhythmical power and variety of this passage, Vaughan has also produced some strong counterpoint, especially in a *sforzando* form (indicated by the stress-marks).

These two same contrasting types of rhythm may also be traced, though rather less sharply, in his octosyllabic couplets and in his quatrains. Compare, for example, the metrically dominated lines of *The Retreat*,

> O how I long to travel back
> And tread again that ancient track!
> That I might once more reach that plain,

Where first I left my glorious train,
From whence th' enlighten'd spirit sees
That shady City of palm-trees, etc.,

with these lines from *The Dwelling-Place* :

Did some cloud
Fix'd to a tent, descend and shroud
My distress'd Lord ? or did a star
Beckon'd by Thee, though high and far,
In sparkling smiles haste gladly down
To lodge light, and increase her own ?

The formal metrical pattern of these two passages is the same; their rhythm—also, of course, diversely conditioned by their sound-texture—is entirely different.

The extract from *The Retreat*, one of Vaughan's best poems, should remind us that rhythm dominated by metrical beat, form, and rhyme is not necessarily inferior to the other type—in the short lyrical poem at any rate. The first type is certainly more prone than the second to monotony and mechanical regularity; but, this danger avoided, it has its own charm—and its own special qualities. It is particularly fitted to the song-like and the incantatory sort of poem; it may create an effect of grace, precision, neatness. There is no reason (except prejudice) why a liking for the more dynamic rhythms of Donne, Hopkins, and much of Vaughan, should render us deaf to those of Herrick, De la Mare, and most of Herbert.

So, while we enjoy the rhythmic tensions of *Regeneration* we should also be able to find delight in the graceful sweetness of *Peace*, which is rhythmically dependent on its metrical form to an extreme degree—none of Vaughan's poems more so :

My soul, there is a country
Far beyond the stars,
Where stands a winged sentry
All skilful in the wars,
There above noise, and danger
Sweet Peace sits crown'd with smiles,
And One born in a manger
Commands the beauteous files,

He is thy gracious Friend,
     And (O my soul awake!)
Did in pure love descend
     To die here for thy sake,
If thou canst get but thither,
     There grows the flower of Peace,
The Rose that cannot wither,
     Thy fortress, and thy ease;
Leave then thy foolish ranges;
     For none can thee secure,
But One, who never changes,
     Thy God, thy life, thy cure.

CHAPTER XII

A RHETORICAL STRAIN

In much of Vaughan's early work, in various incidental passages and in pieces like *A Rhapsodis*, *To Amoret Weeping*, the translation of Juvenal's tenth satire, *The Charnel House*, *In Amicum Foeneratorem*, *To his Friend — —*, *To his Retired Friend*, and *Upon a Cloke lent him by Mr J. Ridsley*, there is a strain of poetry that may perhaps be described as rhetorical—objective, observational writing that is usually directed towards everyday and social life, that is explicit in statement, vigorous (and sometimes violent) in tone, colloquial, humorous, and often generally satirical. This kind of verse was no doubt chiefly inspired, if sometimes through more immediate channels, by 'Great Ben'; it probably owed something to Donne also.

Two illustrations may serve to substantiate the above description, as well as to remind us that there are good things to be found in *Poems* and *Olor Iscanus*. The first passage, a London street scene, which might almost be something out of Dryden, comes from *A Rhapsodis*; the second humorously depicts the physical effects of sleeping naked in Mr Ridsley's old cloak:

[1]
Should we go now a-wand'ring, we should meet
With catchpoles, whores and carts in ev'ry street:
Now when each narrow lane, each nook and cave,
Sign-posts and shop-doors, pimp for ev'ry knave,
When riotous sinful plush, and tell-tale spurs
Walk Fleet Street and the Strand, when the soft stirs
Of bawdy, ruffled silks, turn night to day;
And the loud whip and coach scolds all the way;
When lust of all sorts, and each itchy blood
From the Tower-wharf to Cymbeline, and Lud,
Hunts for a mate, and the tir'd footman reels
'Twixt chairmen, torches, and the hackney wheels. . . .

191

[2]
O that thou hadst been there next morn, that I
Might teach thee new Micro-cosmo-graphy!
Thou wouldst have ta'en me, as I naked stood,
For one of the seven pillars before the flood.
Such characters and hieroglyphics were
In one night worn, that thou mightst justly swear
I'd slept in cere-cloth, or at Bedlam, where
The madmen lodge in straw. . . .
Nay, I believe, had I that instant been
By surgeons or apothecaries seen,
They had condemned my raz'd skin to be
Some walking herbal, or anatomy.

Rhetorical poetry of this kind, though devoid of its gaiety and humour, survives into *Silex Scintillans*, where it remains strongly present along with the predominantly lyrical mode of writing—with poetry, that is to say, of an intimate and confessional kind, powerfully inspired by individual emotion and imagination (whatever the intellectual element), and speaking a language that is intense, richly evocative, and deliberately suggestive. (Incidentally, this marked blend of the rhetorical and lyrical in Vaughan is another characteristic that clearly distinguishes his poetry from Herbert's, where the rhetorical flavour is much less pronounced.) The purest and most sustained example in *Silex Scintillans* of this kind of rhetorical writing is probably *The Proffer*, a poem that is obscure in certain respects but is clearly a sharp, forceful piece of invective occasioned by some attempt to persuade Vaughan into reconciliation, and perhaps collaboration, with the Commonwealth régime :

O pois'nous, subtile fowls!
The flies of hell,
That buzz in every ear, and blow on souls,
Until they smell,
And rot, descend not here, nor think to stay!
I've read, who 'twas drove you away. . . .

No, no; I am not he;
Go seek elsewhere!
I skill not your fine tinsel, and false hair,
Your sorcery,
And smooth seducements : I'll not stuff my story
With your Commonwealth and glory.

Such poetry as this is far removed from *The Morning-Watch* or
'They are all gone into the world of light'; but it stems directly
from much of Vaughan's secular verse, from such lines, for instance, as his denunciation of moneylenders in *In Amicum
Foeneratorem* :

Talk not of shreeves, or gaol;
I fear them not. I have no land to glut
Thy dirty appetite, and make thee strut
Nimrod of acres; I'll no speech prepare
To court the hopeful cormorant, thine heir.

A much more admirable passage, which E. W. Williamson
rightly distinguishes for its 'fine rhetorical sweep',[1] is the middle
and main section of *The World*, with its strong, emblematic[2]
sketches of various types of worldly vanity among the unelect—
of the 'doting Lover', the miser, the epicure, and, most forceful
of all, of the 'darksome Statesman'[3]—

Churches and altars fed him; perjuries
Were gnats and flies;
It rain'd about him blood and tears, but he
Drank them as free.

Several anthologists, following Palgrave's precedent in the
Golden Treasury, have converted this poem into a lyric by print-
ing the first seven lines only (with or without the last fifteen).
This drastic surgery produces a quite attractive, if somewhat
obscure poem.[4] But the lyric so manufactured is not Vaughan's;
and for the ordinary reader who knows the poet only from the

---

[1] *Henry Vaughan*, p. 32. The quoted remark concerns the poem as a whole.
[2] See Rosemary Freeman, *English Emblem Books*, p. 151.
[3] Certainly some Commonwealth leader, possibly Cromwell.
[4] In this opinion I am with Blunden (*On the Poetry of Henry Vaughan*, p. 54) and
in disagreement with the implication of Kermode (*The Private Imagery of Henry
Vaughan*, p. 210).

anthologies the abridgement is to be regretted since it conceals
a tough, coarse-textured rhetorical manner of writing that is
fairly common in *Silex Scintillans*.

Apart from the opening of *Isaac's Marriage*, there are few
other sustained examples in *Silex Scintillans* of this rhetorical
style. But it is to be found fairly often in conjunction with
Vaughan's dominant lyrical mode. For example, in *The Constellation* stanzas like

> Fair, order'd lights—whose motion without noise
> Resembles those true joys
> Whose spring is on that hill, where you do grow,
> And we here taste sometimes below . . .

alternate with such stanzas as

> But here, commission'd by a black self-will,
> The sons the father kill,
> The children chase the mother, and would heal
> The wounds they give, by crying, Zeal.

Again, the conclusion of *St Mary Magdalen*, with its attack on
the pharisaic attitude and its thrust at the rule of the 'Saints'—

> 'This woman'—say'st thou—'is a sinner' :
> And sate there none such at thy dinner ?
> Go, leper, go! wash till thy flesh
> Comes like a child's, spotless and fresh;
> He is still leprous that still paints :
> Who saint themselves, they are no saints

—is in sharp contrast (though not discordantly) with the predominantly lyrical strain of the rest of the poem, with lines like
the opening—

> Dear, beauteous Saint! more white than day
> When in his naked, pure array;
> Fresher than morning-flowers which shew
> As thou in tears dost, best in dew

—or with the lovely image :

> That at the root of this green tree
> Thy great decays restor'd might be.

We may notice, too, how the pedestrian verses of *Rules and Lessons*—quickened also by a few lyrical snatches—are occasionally envigorated by some colloquial, impassioned, rhetorical writing:

> Injure not modest blood, whose spirits rise
> In judgment against lewdness; that's base wit
> That voids but filth and stench. Hast thou no prize
> But sickness or infection? stifle it.
> Who makes his jests of sins, must be at least,
> If not a very devil, worse than a beast.

In the main, though there is very little of it in the greatest poems, this combination of the rhetorical and lyrical produces an harmonious blend. The successful fusion is largely effected by the nature of Vaughan's lyrical style—its vigorous directness, concreteness, idiomatic turns of phrase, and recurrent speech rhythms. Indeed, there are no doubt numerous passages in *Silex Scintillans* where it would be difficult to say whether the writing was primarily rhetorical or lyrical. On the other hand, as for instance in the already discussed fifth stanza of *The Night*, the two modes do sometimes jar a little on the reader.

CHAPTER XIII

THE UNITY AND CONTINUITY OF 'SILEX SCINTILLANS'

THOUGH it consists of one hundred and twenty-nine mainly short poems and is divided into two Parts that were separated by five years in publication, *Silex Scintillans*, like *The Temple*, Shakespeare's Sonnets, *Fleurs du Mal* (and we might add Hopkins' *Poems*) is essentially a poetic *work*, not a collection of miscellaneous lyrics : it makes an impact, perhaps its profoundest impact, as a whole. As Blunden truly says : 'There are many threads and clues which connect the poems of Vaughan and make it more profitable to read his work as a whole than in separate examples.'[1]

One obvious reason for this unity of *Silex Scintillans* is the continuous and predominant devotional nature of the poems; another the fact that they clearly fall into a small number of groups—those on Biblical subjects and personages, on Christ, on the central articles of the Christian faith, on the various Church days and festivals, and on Vaughan's own spiritual progress. Though this last group is an extensive one, it is made up of variations on a limited number of themes,[2] while the elegies and pietistic pieces are most closely related to these devotional groups, often overlapping them. Further, all the poems are bound together by an abundance of imagery drawn from Nature, by frequent Herbert and Scriptural echoes and quotations, and by the continual hermetic allusions and terminology.

Besides these general groupings, there are also six poems in

---

[1] *On the Poems of Henry Vaughan*, p. 24.
[2] See pp. 19–21 and pp. 201–3 *passim*.

Part I that have their complement in Part II[1] and at least half a dozen sequences of closely interrelated poems.[2] The volume begins with such a sequence in the three pieces *Death, Resurrection and Immortality,* and *Day of Judgment.*[3] Two other instances of marked continuity are to be seen in *The Ass, The Hidden Treasure,* and *Childhood,* poems intimately connected by their themes of humility, submission, and renunciation of intellectual inquiry and knowledge, and in the six poems on death and resurrection towards the end of Part II, *The Throne, Death, The Feast, The Obsequies, The Waterfall,* and *Quickness.*

Another link between the poems is the fairly frequent repetition of identical (or near identical) phrases and turns of expression.[4] Admittedly, most of these iterations are slight in effect and may long pass unnoticed by the reader. But one or two of them stand out quite prominently, like the 'homing' idea, which, after its appearance in *Affliction*—

> And brings man home when he doth range

—occurs five times in the next thirteen poems.[5]

[1] *Death: A Dialogue* with *Death; The Retreat* with *Childhood; Holy Scriptures* with *To the Holy Bible, The Holy Communion* with *The Feast, The Constellation* (or perhaps, better, *Midnight*) with *The Star,* and the two *Day of Judgment* poems.

[2] Three examples of close grouping in addition to those mentioned in the text are: *The Shower, Distraction, The Pursuit; Admission, Praise, Dressing, Easter Day, Easter Hymn;* and *Ascension Day, Ascension Hymn,* 'They are all gone into the world of light.'

[3] The poem that precedes this group is *Regeneration.* The theme of *Regeneration* is the quest of God and religion. Vaughan immediately returns to this theme in the two consecutive poems *Religion* and *The Search.*

[4] The fact that many of the most marked of these repetitions—like many of the chief examples of image parallels—are concentrated in small groups of consecutive poems tempts one to guess that most of the pieces in *Silex Scintillans* are probably printed in the order of their original composition. The occasional sequences of related poems point to the same conclusion, for while it is easy to imagine Vaughan from time to time writing several poems round some common theme, it is hard to believe that in the preparation of his mss. for publication he would have brought some related poems together and left other related ones in scattered isolation.

[5] *Retirement,* ll. 10–11; *The Pilgrimage,* l. 8; *The Mutiny,* l. 23 and l. 30; *The Shepherds,* ll. 45–6; and *Man,* l. 19. A similar, though more scattered, example occurs with the 'tracking' of souls in their heavenward flight, an expression Vaughan probably picked up from Habington's *Elegy 3 to Talbot,* ll. 2–3. See *An Elegy on the Death of Mr R. Hall,* ll. 65–6; *Isaac's Marriage,* ll. 48–50; 'Silence and stealth of days,' ll. 23–6; 'I walk'd the other day,' ll. 48–9; *Cock-Crowing,* ll. 33–6; and *To his Books* (*Thalia Rediviva*), l. 4.

Throughout both Parts of *Silex Scintillans* repetitions or cross-echoes of whole lines and passages are also quite common. For instance, there is an obvious resemblance between two lines in 'And do they so?' (a poem in Part I)—

> Can they their heads lift, and expect,
> And groan too?

—and two lines in *Palm Sunday* (which occurs in Part II):

> Trees, flowers, and herbs; birds, beasts, and stones,
> That since man fell, expect with groans
> To see the Lamb....

(Here, of course, the similarity arises from a common echo of Rom. 8. 19 and 22-3.) A more sustained example of such reminiscence is to be found in *Corruption*, where Vaughan's picture of the childhood of man—

> He shin'd a little, and by those weak rays
> Had some glimpse of his birth.
> He saw heaven o'er his head, and knew from whence
> He came, condemned, hither;
> And, as first love draws strongest, so from hence
> His mind sure progress'd thither

—immediately recalls his description in *The Retreat* of his own first years:

> Happy those early days, when I
> Shin'd in my angel-infancy....
> When yet I had not walk'd above
> A mile or two from my first love,
> And looking back—at that short space—
> Could see a glimpse of His bright face.

Occasionally, too, some odd line has the effect of evoking in a flash an entire poem. How immediately, for example, the close of *The Star*, unmistakable Vaughan in every word—

> as herbs unseen
> Put on their youth and green

—calls up his elegy 'I walk'd the other day'; and how beautifully and suggestively epitomised is *The Star* itself by these two lines from *Love-Sick*:

> That Thou wert pleas'd to shed Thy grace so far
> As to make man all pure love, flesh a star!

But perhaps the most striking of all such cross-references is a passage in *Providence*:

> Poor birds this doctrine sing,
> And herbs which on dry hills do spring,
> Or in the howling wilderness
> Do know Thy dewy morning hours,
> And watch all night for mists or showers,
> Then drink and praise Thy bounteousness.

Here the 'poor birds' and their 'doctrine' at once recall the poem *The Bird*, which also deals with the theme of Providence; while the thought of these lines, with some very slight reminiscence of phrase, runs close to that of stanzas two and three in the earlier poem.

However, the most continuous and fundamental link between the poems of *Silex Scintillans*, giving the work a greater unity than *The Temple*, is their common and highly individualised imagery—the very large number of repeated single images, the recurrent image-clusters, and the distinctive 'world' within, and to some extent behind, the poems, turning perpetually to its elemental rhythm of light and darkness, daybreak and night. Outstanding as this kind of cohesion is, it requires no further stressing here, for it has already been sufficiently discussed. But perhaps two further relevant points may be briefly made. First, because there is this unmistakable Vaughan world and because it is so richly epitomised in his masterpieces, these poems act in an exceptional way as nodal points for the whole work. They are filamented, so to speak, to a large number of inferior pieces —the scattered rough sketches for the concentrated finished picture.[1] Secondly, those fragmentary lines and half lines of surprising exceptional beauty that so often light up Vaughan's mediocre poems (this is of course one of the main features of his

---

[1] See the remarks on *The Morning-Watch*, pp. 131–2, and the footnote references on p. 132.

work)[1] are not merely redeeming 'fine phrases' in the usual sense of that term, admirable epithets, metaphors, etc.: they often have the effect, which contributes to the unity of *Silex Scintillans*, of instantly transporting us into the centre of his imaginative world.

It must be admitted that these repetitions of theme, phrasing, and to some extent of imagery expose the limitations of Vaughan's poetry. To put the criticism simply, he is a writer of narrow, though intensely cultivated, experience who does sometimes rather repeat himself. But, paradoxically, these limitations of the poet are a source of strength to his book, for his repetitions (which rarely approach monotony and never poverty, a different matter) certainly help to make his collection of lyrics a unified whole. Had he been more widely ranging and inventive, *Silex Scintillans* would obviously have been richer and more varied in appeal; but, almost as certainly, it would have lost much of its coherence as a work.

Much the same could probably be said of *A Shropshire Lad*, written by a poet far more limited than Vaughan. Many nineteenth- and twentieth-century collections of lyrics contain poems that are greatly superior to anything Housman ever wrote. For instance, nothing in *A Shropshire Lad* approaches *Poem in October* or *Fern Hill* in Dylan Thomas's volume *Deaths and Entrances*; yet it can hardly be denied that *A Shropshire Lad* strikes us as a unified whole in a way that *Deaths and Entrances* —or, for that matter, Thomas's *Collected Poems*—do not. And this total effect in a volume of lyrical poems is a real aesthetic sensation that does count for something.

While *Silex Scintillans* has thus a considerable degree of unity, its two Parts are clearly distinct in tone; and it is obvious that the five years separating their publication mark a discernible stage in Vaughan's spiritual development.

Reading Part I, which is appropriately introduced by a key

[1] Cf. Mrs Joan Bennett, *Four Metaphysical Poets*, p. 85: 'a selection from the best of Vaughan would include some single stanzas, lines, or even half lines.'

poem on regeneration, we have a strong impression of a struggle for assured faith and salvation, of spiritual unquiet, conflict, and often of deep anguish. There are certainly intervals of joy and serenity, captured in such poems as *The Morning-Watch* and *Peace*; but these moments are rare. The main, and characteristic, themes are death,[1] the spiritual quest (and its complement, apathy, back-sliding, and distraction), the desperate need for repentance, and the value of affliction. There is also considerable emphasis on the Fall of man, and, parallel with this, an extreme stress on the poet's own sinfulness, worthlessness, and vileness:

> In all this round of life and death
> Nothing's more vile than is my breath;
> Profaneness on my tongue doth rest,
> Defects and darkness in my breast;
> Pollutions all my body wed,
> And even my soul to Thee is dead.

Repentance

Typical and indicative titles, not to be matched in Part II, are: *The Search, Distraction, The Storm, The Relapse, The Mutiny, Misery.*

Unquestionably we should be distorting Part II if we forced it into a sharp and continuous antithesis with Part I. Just as the first Part has its moments of joy, so the second, in such poems as *Love-Sick, Begging,* and *Anguish,* rings at times with the old note of self-condemnation and a deeply troubled spirit. Nevertheless, the characteristic themes of the first volume are less prominent in the second, and in so far as they remain they are often handled in a very different way. For instance, the subject of death (as we may see by comparing the two poems of that name, one in each Part) is treated much more in a spirit of calm assurance than in the agitation of one hungry for reassurance: turning away from mortality, physical corruption, and from resurrection as a doctrine, Vaughan's attention is more steadily settled on the bliss of the life hereafter; he yearns for heaven

---

[1] It will be noticed that most of the elegies come in Part I.

rather than hopes for it. That is why 'They are all gone into the world of light', characterised by such lines as

> Dear, beauteous Death! the jewel of the just,

belongs to Part II as it never could to Part I.

But there is a positive change between the two Parts even more striking than the negative. The opening lines of Part II,

> Lord Jesus! with what sweetness and delights,
> Sure, holy hopes, high joys, and quick'ning flights,
> Dost Thou feed Thine![1]

—indeed the whole of this first poem—truly intimates the prevailing mood of the volume. As we read on, we feel that the prayer in the penultimate poem of Part I—

> Show me Thy peace,
> Thy mercy, love, and ease

—has been largely answered. Though Vaughan is still at times wrung with pangs of remorse for his old sinful ways—

> Yet joy itself will make a right soul grieve
> To think he should be so long vainly led;
> *The Timber*

—in a number of poems we now feel that his spiritual night—to say nothing of his earlier unregenerate days—is more of a recollection than a present actuality. He has found God for certain:

> But I am sure Thou dost now come
> Oft to a narrow, homely room,
> Where Thou too hast but the least part;
> My God, I mean my sinful heart;
> *The Dwelling-Place*

and with the finding of God, this sense of His presence, he has discovered true joy and a serener, more balanced attitude:

---

[1] For another example of the repeated phrases we may note that 'holy hopes, high joys' is followed in the next poem but one by 'O holy hope! and high humility'. There is also some slight resemblance between the first two lines of the quotation and the opening of *The Morning-Watch*.

> Thou hast
> Another mirth, a mirth, though overcast
> With clouds and rain, yet full as calm and fine
> As those clear heights which above tempests shine.
>
> *Joy*

This new attitude is admirably reflected in *The Bird*, a poem which—though of course without any warrant from Vaughan—we might read as an allegory of his own spiritual history :

> Many a sullen storm
> For which coarse man seems much the fitter born,
> Rain'd on thy bed
> And harmless head.
>
> And now as fresh and cheerful as the light
> Thy little heart in early hymns doth sing
> Unto that Providence, Whose unseen arm
> Curb'd them, and cloth'd thee well and warm.

Mingled with this joy, assurance, and serenity in Part II there is still an intense note of spiritual distress. But Vaughan's anguish now is not so much for his shortcomings and sinfulness as for the frustration of this 'false' mortal existence to one 'love-sick' for home and the true life. Further, though he has found God, he suffers, as never before, the pangs of separation from Him, the intermittency of the vision, and the sense of obscuring veils hung between himself and the Divine Light. This is the lament we hear continually in Part II, in lines like :

> O Thy bright looks! Thy glance of love
> Shown, and but shown, me from above!
> Rare looks! that can dispense such joy
> As without wooing wins the coy,
> And makes him mourn, and pine, and die,
> Like a starv'd eaglet, for Thine eye.
>
> *The Favour*

There are also two smaller changes to be noticed in Part II. The first, already apparent in some of the last poems of Part I like *The World*, *The Constellation*, and *Man*, is a slight shift away from preoccupation with his own spiritual condition to that of mankind in general—a shift that can be seen, for instance, if we compare the two opening poems of each volume. Certainly in *Regeneration* Vaughan has an eye for the state of mankind, as in *Ascension-Day* he is much concerned about the reality and significance of Christ's rising for himself. But for all his ecstatic self-projection into the event he is describing, his *Ascension-Day* is, as a whole, a more objective poem than *Regeneration*.

Secondly, the poems in Part II are distinguished by a more evident spirit of humility and submissiveness. In particular—as we may see from the sequence *The Ass*, *The Hidden Treasure*, and *Childhood*—Vaughan has abandoned the 'search' in so far as it involves intellectual probing, speculation, and argument—even, one may sometimes suspect, among the congenial ideas of hermetic philosophy. He is prepared to rest on faith instead of reason:

> Grant I may soft and lowly be,
> And mind those things I cannot see;
> Tie me to faith, though above reason;
> Who question Power, they speak treason:
> Let me, Thy ass, be only wise
> To carry, not search, mysteries.
> Who carries Thee, is by Thee led;
> Who argues, follows his own head.

The Ass

A few random quotations might be used to prove anything; but the representative nature of those just given can be demonstrated to a certain extent by comparing some of the parallel poems of Parts I and II.

Consider, for example, the two *Day of Judgment* poems. The first, the utterance of a man newly awakened, or re-awakened, to the prospect of spiritual damnation, is a violent, agitated piece of writing in which the main stress is on destruction and on the terror of 'Too late':

> Repentance there is out of date,
> And so is Mercy too.

With this appalling prospect in front of him Vaughan cries out for the penitential scourge of affliction. In the second poem, on the other hand—a lyric fairly summarised by its opening line,

O day of life, of light, of love!

—all that troubled, almost frantic note has died away. Sin, and
even the Judgment itself, is but lightly touched on; filled now
with the thought of resurrection and 'all things new' instead of
destruction, of the Divine love and mercy instead of punishment,
Vaughan yearns for the day that he had once dreaded :

> O come! arise! shine! do not stay,
> Dearly lov'd day!
> The fields are long since white, and I
> With earnest groans for freedom cry.

In place of the flame, thunder, and blast of the first poem, we
have an imagery dominated by light; and while Vaughan is still
not prepared to entertain a conception of illimitable Divine
mercy, he thinks of punishment falling on the Puritans for their
'forgeries' and 'impious wit' rather than on sinners like himself,
'all filth and obscene'.[1]

Another revealing pair of poems is *The Constellation* (Part
I) and *The Star* (Part II). In the first Vaughan uses the stars to
paint, by way of contrast, a depressing picture of the state of
man—his disobedience, distraction, spiritual sloth and blindness,
his lusts, his errors leading to bloodshed, and his persecution of
the true Church. The stars—and heaven—are very far away :

> Fair order'd lights—whose motion without noise
> Resembles those true joys
> Whose spring is on that hill, where you do grow,
> And we here taste sometimes below. . . .

In the Part II counterpart of this poem the stars, no longer
remote but bound to earth in magnetic sympathy, intimate the
hope of union between God and the soul. Joy and beauty,
Vaughan now suggests, are possible even in this mortal life; and
where in the previous poem his emphasis had been on the
spiritual blindness of man—

[1] *Christ's Nativity*, l. 23.

> He gropes beneath here, and with restless care,
> First makes, then hugs a snare;
> Adores dead dust, sets heart on corn and grass,
> But seldom doth make heav'n his glass

—now, much more optimistically, he stresses man's spiritual potentialities :

> For where desire, celestial, pure desire,
> Hath taken root, and grows, and doth not tire,
> There God a commerce states, and sheds
> His secret on their heads.

There is one detail common to both poems that significantly underlines their difference. In the first Vaughan takes up a word much in use in Commonwealth days—'commission'—and, thinking of the Roundheads, gives it a pessimistic, ironic twist :

> But here, commission'd by a black self-will,
> The sons the father kill.

The same word recurs in *The Star*, but it is disinfected now of all bitterness and harmonises with a fundamental optimistic faith instead of denying it :

> Yet, seeing all things that subsist and be,
> Have their commissions from Divinity. . . .

On the other hand, it would be unsound to generalise too widely from these contrasting pairs of poems. For one thing, while the two *Day of Judgment* poems are almost antithetical, there is also another poem on the same theme in Part I, *The Dawning*, that comes very close in spirit to the *Day of Judgment* of Part II. Again, among the remaining pairs of parallel poems (excluding the two on Death),[1] it is only the pair dealing with the Bible that reflects anything of that general spiritual development of Vaughan that we have described. Where in his earlier sonnet, *Holy Scriptures*, he had been preoccupied with his 'hard heart', praising the Bible as a means to his personal salvation, in his second poem he sees his worst sinfulness in retrospect; and

---

[1] As indicated on p. 201 this pair of poems also reveals some significant differences between the two Parts of *Silex Scintillans*.

he now believes that his salvation has been largely achieved, thanks in a great measure to the Scriptures :

> Fruition, union, glory, life,
> Thou didst lead to, and still all strife.
> Living, thou wert my soul's sure ease,
> And dying mak'st me go in peace.

However, there is little notable difference to be observed between *The Holy Communion* and *The Feast*, while *The Retreat* and *Childhood* both express the same Christian—not Wordsworthian—attitude to infancy. If anything, *Childhood* is a sadder, not to say more pessimistic, poem than *The Retreat*, for while the early, happy days of innocence, purity, and vision seem further away, unattainable even in imagination, Vaughan is now also much more conscious of the vanity of adult experience.

But, as we have already said, such notes as these in Part II do not seriously affect the general picture of Vaughan's spiritual development, which could never have followed a simple, continuous, geometric line. Part II is both a continuation from Part I and distinct from it, though we must not exaggerate the differences.

CHAPTER XIV

CLOUDED STAR

As we began this book by considering Vaughan's sudden, and
most striking, realisation of himself as a poet, it is fitting to
end it with some comment on his even more abrupt lapse into
poetic silence after the publication of the second Part of *Silex
Scintillans*.

Not that the silence was absolute, for many years later, in
1678, he brought out a further volume of poems, *Thalia Rediviva*. Of the pieces written between 1655 and 1678 the most
impressive is his pastoral elegy *Daphnis*,[1] which commemorates
the death of his twin brother in 1666; and a passage like the
following may offer some evidence that the poet in him was not
quite extinct in his middle age :

> I heard last May—for May is still high Spring—
> The pleasant Philomel her vespers sing.
> The green wood glitter'd with the golden sun,
> And all the west like silver shin'd; not one
> Black cloud; no rags, nor spots did stain
> The welkin's beauty; nothing frown'd like rain.
> But ere night came, that scene of fine sights turn'd
> To fierce dark show'rs; the air with lightnings burn'd. . . .

One line here in particular—'The green wood glitter'd with the
golden sun'—vibrates with all his old sensibility and magic, and
the last phrase in the quoted passage is an impressively vivid one.

But *Thalia Rediviva* is mainly a collection of old poems be-
longing to the *Silex Scintillans* period and earlier, and, apart

---

[1] Blunden's estimate of Daphnis as an 'uneven but graceful elegy' (*On the Poetry
of Henry Vaughan*, p. 38) is surely much nearer the mark than Beeching's description of it as 'the most formally successful of all Vaughan's performances' (Introduction to the *Muses Library* ed., p. xxxiii).

208

from *Daphnis*, its best pieces are the rejects from *Silex Scintillans*, grouped under the title *Pious Thoughts and Ejaculations*.
Even *Daphnis*, as Hutchinson suggested,[1] may be the re-writing
of a work that was originally composed for the death of the
poet's younger brother in 1648. The new poems that can be
confidently ascribed to the period 1655–78 are few and quite
undistinguished.

Vaughan's eclipse as a poet is probably easier to account for
than his surprising emergence. By 1655 he had passed through
his regenerative period, and the quarrel with himself—that
quarrel that Yeats considered to be the essential inspiration of
all important lyrical poetry—was largely over. After his doubts,
frustrations, backslidings, and conflicts, he had at last found God
and a serenity of mind. He rested, assured, on the central Christian beliefs; and he was drawn towards an unspeculating, un-
questioning attitude of childlike faith. What, in the lyrical
religious vein of most of *Silex Scintillans*, was he to write about
—without repeating himself?[2]

Though, as we have seen, he had some talent for a rhetorical
kind of poetry, he apparently had no inclination or ambition
towards the long, objective sort of religious poem that might
have led him to his *Davideis* or *Hind and the Panther*. He was
born at the wrong time for Wordsworth's sustaining Romantic
belief in poetry as a vocation or destiny; and there are no
grounds for thinking that he ever felt that interest in poetry as a
craft that might have kept him industriously, if unspectacularly,
engaged in verse writing through the long remaining years of
his life. Further, with the deep longing for spiritual calm that is
so prominent in the second Part of *Silex Scintillans*, he may have
decided that the agitation and excitement of poetic composition
was something best avoided.

Again, as was suggested in the first chapter, when we were

---

[1] *Henry Vaughan*, pp. 220–1.
[2] Some of the rejected *Silex Scintillans* poems in *Thalia Rediviva* (*Pious Thoughts
and Ejaculations*) show that Vaughan was indeed beginning to repeat himself.

considering his sudden flowering as a poet, the relationship between his imagination, deeply subconscious in much of its activity, and the organised, created poem was an unusually delicate and precarious one that often broke down and might conceivably at some time break down altogether. To re-state this point in the simplest, summary way, is it after all so surprising that a poet who often came off only in odd lines and short passages should one day lapse into complete silence?

Apart from these personal factors, there is also the climate of the mid-seventeenth century to be taken into account. In the Preface to his *Poems*, in which he speaks of 'these dull times' and 'the dregs of an Age', Vaughan writes: 'I know the years, and what coarse entertainment they afford poetry';[1] and this sentiment, extensively repeated in his poem *To the Editor of the matchless Orinda*, is also echoed in his brother's dedicatory lines to *Olor Iscanus*:

> And though this sullen age possessèd be
> With some strange Desamour to Poetry. . . .
>> *Upon the following Poems*

No doubt, in remarks like these, the twin brothers were chiefly letting off some of their pent-up feelings against the triumph of Puritanism. But if they were prejudiced and also mistaken in the cause of the situation, it certainly appears from Milton's poetic hibernation at this time, from the unfulfilled promise and long silence of Cowley between his *Mistress* (1647) and *Pindaric Odes* (1663), from the decline of Marvell, and the markedly changing direction of these two latter poets, that there was indeed something in the life of the 1640's and 1650's that made poetry writing extremely difficult. Part of the trouble, as the careers of these three poets show, was the urgent demand of public affairs; part of it the general unsettled air of the times—the atmosphere that Cowley indicated in his famous epigram, 'a warlike, various, and tragical age is best to write of, but worst to write in.' But vastly more consequential than all this, though

[1] *Works*, p. 2.

largely concealed from the eyes of its contemporaries, was the tremendous historical revolution that was being effected—the final defeat of a way of life that we may roughly call the mediaeval and the triumphant emergence of the modern. Without any exaggeration we may say that it was Vaughan's fate to be born in one world and to die in another.

Obviously this momentous revolution, in which our twentieth-century world originates, cannot be adequately summarised in a few sentences; and any longer discussion of it would be out of place in this final chapter.[1] Sufficient here to say that it necessitated a radical poetic revolution in which writers embraced new conceptions about the purpose and language of poetry and came to terms with the new, dominant modes of rationalism, specialisation, and of independent fields of thought and inquiry, with religion separated from philosophy, science, and a non-religious life generally, poetry from prose, imagination and fancy from reason and wit, poetic 'truth' (if truth at all) from other forms of truth, and so on. Vaughan's poetry in *Silex Scintillans* was deeply, firmly, and complexly rooted in the old traditional ways of life and thought (much more so than Cowley's early work was, for instance); and it is not surprising that the book received little contemporary recognition. Ignored beyond a small circle of friends and acquaintances, and living at a time when the Romantic conception of poetry writing as a private spiritual diary was unknown, Vaughan can have felt little inducement to compose further poetry of the *Silex Scintillans* kind, while, unlike Cowley and Marvell, he was unable, or unwilling, to adapt himself as a poet to the tastes of a new age[2]—to the world of the 'Restoration', only half a dozen years away from the publication of the second Part of *Silex Scintillans*, that must have been as uncongenial to him as the Common-

[1] Of the innumerable books on this subject see especially, for its special reference to Vaughan, Bethell's *The Cultural Revolution of the Seventeenth Century*.

[2] Outside Vaughan's poetry writing there seems to have been some adjustment. Like Cowley he appears to have interested himself in the more scientific natural history of the second half of the century. There is an interesting remark in his letter to Aubrey (*Works*, p. 672) that probably points to a change of direction: 'If in my attendance upon (rather than speculations into) Nature. . . .'

wealth. He was a defeated, old-fashioned poet as well as a defeated, old-fashioned Royalist. But, though the word meant little to the new age, before defeat he had known his hour of 'glory', when, filled with dreams of 'Paradise and light', he had sometimes found imperishable words for his visions.

INDEX

The four major poems forming the subject of Part II of this book are reproduced in full and studied in detail on the pages given in bold type.